NEW POETRY FROM THE MIDWEST

2014

NEW POETRY FROM THE MIDWEST 2014

OKLA ELLIOTT & HANNAH STEPHENSON
Series Editors

LEE ANN RORIPAUGH
Final Judge of the Heartland Poetry Prizes

newamericanpress
Milwaukee, Wis. • Urbana, Ill.

newamericanpress

www.NewAmericanPress.com

Printed in the United States of America

ISBN 978-1-941561-01-0

For ordering information, please contact:
Ingram Book Group
One Ingram Blvd.
La Vergne, TN 37086
(800) 937-8000
orders@ingrambook.com

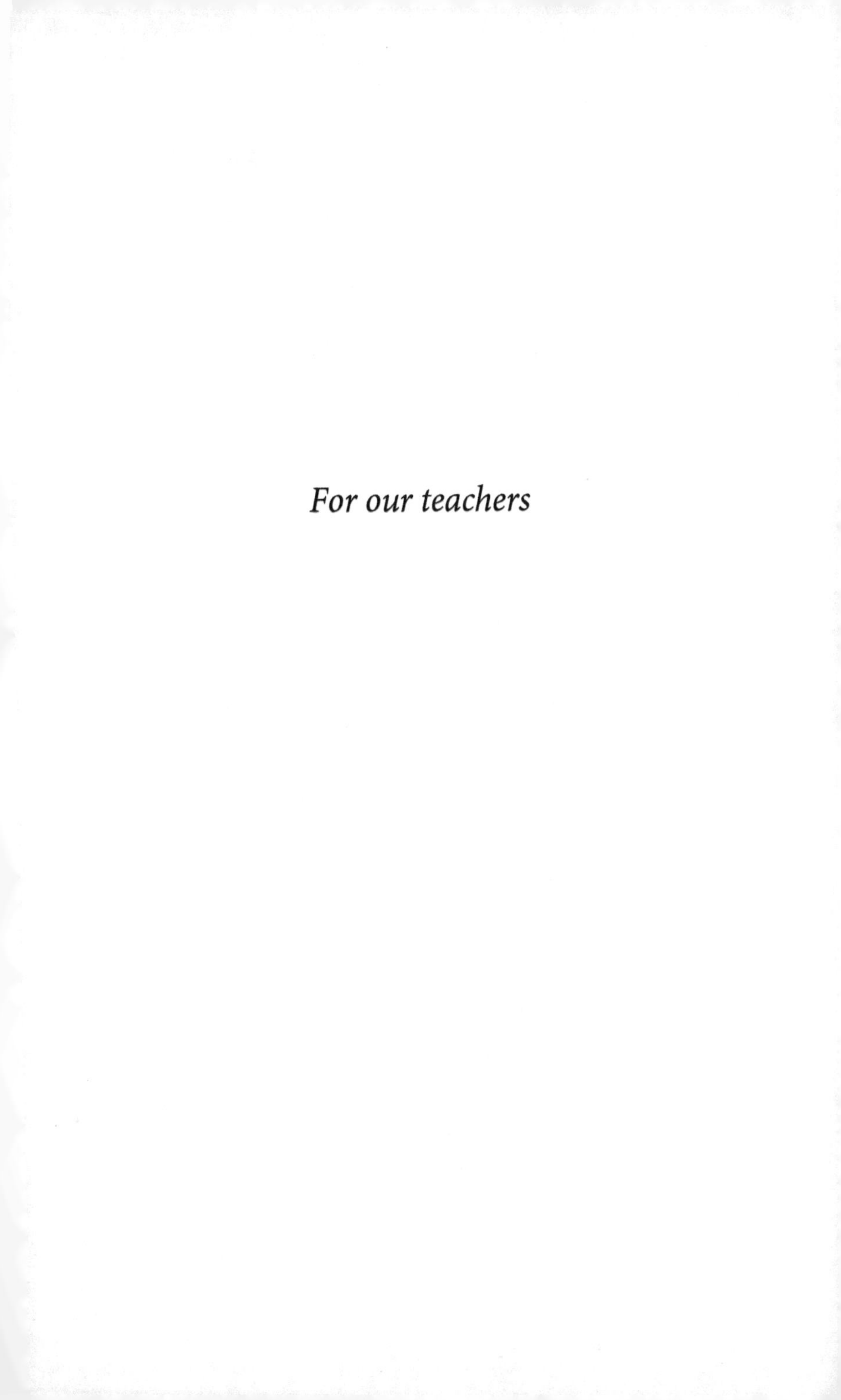

For our teachers

2015 HEARTLAND POETRY PRIZE WINNERS

"Love Like Samson's Lion
While My Mother Shaves
My Father's Head"

by Ruth Awad

"Begin not with coastline,
not with harbor
or cove. Begin"

by Monica Berlin and Beth Marzoni

"Honey"

by Carlo Matos

CONTENTS

Against/Toward Taxonomy:
An Introduction to
New Poetry from the Midwest

It's an exciting time to be a writer living in the Midwest. There are remarkable things happening in our region—and in the poems we selected for this anthology.

We are so proud of and dazzled by *New Poetry from the Midwest*. What makes it Midwestern? We did not select solely, or even predominantly, along lines of content. The poets featured here have some connection to one of the twelve states in the region; they were born here or currently live here or pursued an education here.

An anthology of poems with overtly Midwestern-themed content might make us grimace in anticipation of pastoral cliché and fake "Our state fair is a great state fair" pomp and circumstance. Instead, we selected poems wildly diverse in style, voice, and content.

Let's get this out of the way. Sure, there are animals. Our regional menagerie includes innumerable birds, horses, a 'possum, a neighbor's dog, jackals and a chicken, a python in a grand piano, an elephant, llamas, and a tiny dragon. And there are cornfields and forests, and no shortage of growing things—birches, green grass, acorns, milkweed, children, anger, forgiveness, lust. But there are also cityscapes, imagined worlds, and international concerns; formal verse, free verse, and poems that defy taxonomic efforts altogether.

What does a Midwestern poem sound like? We concede that there is an earnestness that may glisten on the skin of many of these poems. But, thankfully, this collection resists cohesiveness at every turn. Here's what these poems are not: shy, demure, polite, nice-for-the-sake-of-being-nice, simplistic, predictable, wholesome. On one page you'll find Jennifer Jackson Berry, pulling you close to murmur, "We stopped short of kissing, never / even practicing on fists in front of each other." And then there's the skittery humor of Tyler Gobble, who commands, "Get off the internet. It's your birthday, America."

Many of these poems want to catalog and categorize, to make sense of (or revel in) disorder. Think *Farmer's Almanac* gone berserk, a field guide for the subconscious. Nin Andrews presents to us a "Glossary of Deirdres," while Catie Crabtree introduces us to a machine gun woman, an airplane woman, a submarine woman. In "A Taxonomy of the Space between Us," Caleb Curtiss offers, "This is a poem about me and my brother; about how the space between us is neither division nor connection."

Sandy Longhorn claims that "Nothing is haunted...in quite the way small Midwestern farms / are haunted." We tend to agree. Ghosts loom large in these poems. Are ghosts Midwestern? Maybe—at very least, the Midwest skews toward the spooky and magical. A girl turns into a bird; a man swallows spiders and sparrows. Oz makes two cameo appearances. Peter Davis's sassy Emily Dickinson returns from the dead to say, "Talk to the hand!"

Honest, broken-hearted, or devilishly playful, these poems want to invite you in. Forget pleasantries and small talk—the poets in this anthology offer you heaping servings of sincerity, strangeness, and startling perspectives. They at once embody and explode our notions of the Midwest. We hope you enjoy reading them as much as we have.

— Okla Elliott and Hannah Stephenson

Series Editors

LINDSEY ALEXANDER

* * *

Saudades [Bottle Rocket]

Kiddo, halt this bottle rocket. Cork its mouth
so the ideas don't lose their flavor while no one's listening.

Some men say the soul's a circle,
                                        and it's possible, sure, that souls could work
like Venn Diagrams' overlapping or like
horoscope charts.
          (Coincidence sometimes feels so fateful,
so fatal.) But mine's more a line extending out farther,
farther from me—
                    an arrowhead at both ends, shooting.

That's how growing feels—like the man accused
of witchcraft, strapped to the pressing rack, *more weight, more weight*—
                    a stretch toward death.

Recall the lion that has a man position his head inside its mouth, slowly:
the beast that won't bite down.
                                Consider the will Aesop's lion exerts
                                in not eating the mouse.

  Or the insistent modesty of a brown dwarf star:
                                        one that fails
      to ignite, only detectable by its gravitational pull.

*

For some time, I replaced my bedtime prayers
with the steady counting of worries.
But things have changed.
>   When now I lay me down to sleep,
I request that if I'm good, I'll come back
as a horseshoe,
>   feeling the ground for the horse
because the horse ought not to feel it.

FROM Crazyhorse

LINDSEY ALEXANDER

* * *

Where I Think I Might Belong

A diorama: Here are the stars of foil, here
the tiny workbench, there the cloud, the grass,
the river moving fast, and there is tiny me
set here just plain: knob-head, yellow yarn me.

We are dogs on leashes, her and me. We're dots
on grids: A4 when she leans on the toothpick fence
at the shoebox edge, D3: me searching shelves for glue
that will keep her house from pulling apart; my hand

pulling through tiny me's hair. In the box, there's no
early morning, or birds going south—there's no song
at all except what I sing myself. A stone
in the river or a cat swimming circles over

my blue cellophane body of water. Close the lid
on my box, and tiny me swims like that,
too. She doesn't like taking her clothes off
in front of me. When we dream, we dream

about how scythes spin, and lassoes in old Westerns.
A helicopter's blades spin, but also its wheels and also
gauges inside of it. Unlike the birds that aren't
in the box, I don't know much about flight.

*

But if I lift the box, it's like tiny me is flying.
Words have a sweet spot in the box's corner,
memorizable index card wonders: *subdue, substantiate,*
subsume—the field in the shoebox and the field

with gray sky pressing it flatter can fulfill these
words, we think. My dog made of corks and my papier-mâché
hill, and my dog lying beside the radiator—they
all are plotted by some sort of coordinates, too.

FROM FORKLIFT, OHIO

* * *

A Glossary of Deirdres

Alpha Deirdre:

The first Deirdre I remember. She stood on the steps of Rayen High School in Youngstown, Ohio, a strap of her dress gliding off one shoulder.

Après-Deirdre:

My life after Deirdre. Also, the term I use to refer to all the women I dated after Deirdre left me. She's an après-D., I'd sigh to myself.

Deirdre, the Babe:

Deirdre, the Babe, dressed in red leather boots and nothing else, just for me. Deirdre? I asked. Yes, she answered when I reached for her slender waist. Yes!

Clairvoyant Deirdre:

She kept watching me, evaluating me, telling my life story, long before I lived it. And after.

Contrite Deirdre:

Deirdre when she folded back into herself like a fan.

Devout Deirdre:

At night when she called out, God, Oh God, I answered all her prayers.

Effervescent Deirdre:

A narcotic I wanted to inject into my veins.

Evasive Deirdre:

Glancing down or away whenever I asked her questions, she took to wearing sunglasses day and night.

Felicific Deirdre:

She manifested happiness with her tongue, her fingers, her lips.

Fictional Deirdre:

The Deirdre I told my friends and family about.

Ghost-Deirdre:

The Deirdre who appeared whenever I was in the arms of another woman.

Heavenly Deirdre:

A barely detectable feeling that swam in my blood for years, like minnows flipping their tails, swishing beneath my skin.

Ignescent Deirdre:

A flammable Deirdre. A Deirdre who let off sparks wherever she walked.

Illusions of Deirdre:

All the women who looked like Deirdre until I called out, Deirdre!

Jealous Deirdre:

She dragged me through the mud like a pair of old shoes. This, I once thought, is true love.

Karmic Deirdre:

Like a casualty I could not avoid, Deirdre became my past, my present, my future.

Kinky Deirdre:

She still visits me in dreams. Go away! I tell her. She smiles and ties a silk leash around my neck.

Lazy Deirdre:

Her long hair spilling over her shoulders like a river of red silk, she slept the weekends away on the living room couch.

Long-winded Deirdre:

The Deirdre who became more desirable in absentia.

Mellow Deirdre:

A late night Deirdre who melted like butter on hot toast.

Mystical Deirdre:

Deirdre in bed. Also, the Deirdre who could make a slave of any man.

Nude Deirdre:

Also niveous Deirdre, or Deirdre in nothing but her snowy white skin.

Obsessive Deirdre:

She removed my hair, one strand at a time. One day when I looked in the mirror, a strange, bald man stared back.

Peachy Deirdre:

She was so soft and juicy, she came on her own.

Queen Deirdre; also *Quim Deirdre*:

Both queen and quim were words Deirdre used to address her vagina.

Quarrelsome Deirdre:

She glared at me as if to ask, Is that the best you can do?

Reheated Deirdre:

In the end leftovers were all we had.

Repentant Deirdre:

Can we begin again? she sobbed, the tears falling fast.

Silent Deirdre:

What's the matter? I asked. She said nothing. After a while the nothing surrounded us like a winter night.

Thieving Deirdre:

She stole tiny pieces of me, so tiny I didn't notice a thing at first. One day I woke, late and alone, in an empty house and discovered I, too, was missing.

Unbidden Deirdre:

Leave! I said whenever I saw her lurking around my mind. She came closer and closer until all I could see was Deirdre.

Vanishing Deirdre:

What is it that you want? I asked as she strode away in her red leather boots without a backward glance, the clip, clip of her heels the only sound.

Wonderful Deirdre:

A theoretical Deirdre I remember so well. Also, the Deirdre stolen by another man.

Wanting Deirdre:

Even when I did not want her, I could feel the feeling of wanting her. And I wanted her.

Xenophobe Deirdre:

She hated strangers, or any men who failed to admire her, and any women who admired me.

Yawning Deirdre:

The Deirdre who preferred reading People Magazine and watching Dallas to making love. Also, the Deirdre who faked her orgasms.

The Yin and Yang of Deirdre:

The coarse and the smooth, the meek and the mad, the unyielding and the lissome, the eternal and the lost. All were my Deirdre, and none were my Deirdre.

Zaftig Deirdre:

A full-bodied Deirdre who sends Christmas cards with photos and a few lines, telling how she is living happily ever after. She never admits how often she dials my number, letting it ring and ring. I never admit how afraid I am to answer her calls.

FROM PoetsArtists

* * *

I Was Given a Tiny Dragon

folded from gold foil—origami; gift from a barkeep
like a secret wizard, his beard a dirty river.

Of the two German words I know
wizard is one (Hexenmeister); the other signifies

a process carried out in imagination only
(gedankenexperiment) rather

than performed in the real world.

Oh, the infinite
number of times

I have closed my eyes
to unbutton your shirt, sliding

each little disc free from its hole
as deliberately as letting

a river swallow

tossed stones. So many things
I would put in a box labeled

*

what I want to do to you: what it is like to be hungry
and open the door

to a dark room filled entirely with apples.
Through the window, slice

of the cold moon.

FROM Court Green

ROBERT ARCHAMBEAU

* * *

Nag Hammadi: A Parable

It's night: the watchman discovers a thief in the fields.
They fight, the thief is slain, but his kinsman kills the watchman in revenge.
The watchman's sons find the dead thief's kinsman selling molasses
    in the market.

They hack him to pieces with their mattocks. They eat his heart. It's day.
It's true—it's Egypt, 1945. No one would speak against them—
some silent from fear, some choked with hatred of the dead man and his kin.

Months pass. The watchman's sons stalk slowly through dry hills.
They find a cave, and a red jar, very old.
Is it heavy with gold? Does it cage a demon?

The elder brother conjures courage, hoists his mattock, smashes down.
Below the whirling dust are 13 books—cracked and ancient, without sense
(no one taught these brothers how to read). Books hiss as kindling in
    their mother's oven.

By chance, a Coptic priest comes. He saves what few remain.
They are relics of the bygone Gnostics—the Apocyphon of James,
 the Tripartite Tractate, the Treatise on the Resurrection.

They have nothing in common but this: each declares the evil of this world.

FROM CULTURAL SOCIETY

{ 33 }

RUTH AWAD

* * *

Love Like Samson's Lion While My Mother Shaves My Father's Head

She takes my glasses and our edges blur—
Asiatic hide, blighted wings,
honeycomb.

> The blade down his scalp like running through
> a field where night grows tall
> on thin black stalks.

Locks fall to my lap like seeds. I hear a hundred bees
milling, dragging
their static.

> His mane on the floor like clods of dirt.
> The dark bulb of my heart
> takes root.

My mouth is a cave, words swarm
amber and belligerent,
warm and curling.

> My fingers in his hair, I feel
> only the heat
> of a bruise.

*

My love is like a bee circling
the incisor of a
jawbone—

then let me be the milkweed
sharpening
its toxin.

FROM *ANTI*-

DAVID BAKER

* * *

On Arrogance

I thought I
killed it—too
    little water. Too much sunlight.
    Wrong pot: bad plan: what-

ever. So
says my girl, when it's all too much
    to deal with. A
    difficult thing's easier

to dismiss these
days than
    face. I know. I hung
    three ferns on the porch so she would

find it homey, like home had been,
and I would too.
    Who knew
    the robins started there in stealth?

By the time
I saw their nest the fern
    was sickly gray, a
    maw in the middle of fronds

*

splayed like shocked hair.
Twice I poured
    my spout of water beneath
    the nest; got buzzed, cussed, harped at

from the power line running
from the porch.
    Whatever. I let them go, and they were born.
    I hoisted neighbor kids for

a look—tiny brown
puddle of bodies in a cup,
    bubble eyes, splayed beaks, such
    rapt new hunger—

but not Kate: not
interested. I took
    photos to show. Not Kate.
    They grew, and then—one on a Tuesday,

the next two
the next day—they flew.
    I hear her calling across long
    shadows of green yards

some days, or think
I do. Today
    it was the cat
    at the screen door, yowling to get back in—

and him with a mouthful
of bird. Good boy.
    He dropped it at my feet
    and stood there

unblinking upward, wanting
his simple scratch, and all I could think
    was Jesus, David, now
    what have you done?

FROM AMERICAN POETRY REVIEW

DAVID BAKER

* * *

What Is a Weed?

1.

Emerald, as in the leaf of the ash,
though nothing's burned, not yet, as the ash-green,
gray-green fiery wingspan of the adult
whose bullet body and "flat black eyes" are
less the way we know them than by the trees,
by the death of the trees, by the millions.
The adults emerge, a. planipennis
(of the genus Agrilus), in May, June,
July, then in bark crevices, between
layers of the diamond derma, females
set their eggs whose larvae, in a week, bore
back into the trees. They chew the phloem.
They eat the inner body of the bark,
creating winding galleries as they feed.
This "cuts the flow" of water nutrients
to the tree. This "causes dieback," causes death.

2.

What is a weed? What I saw was a tree.
A thousand trees in the village, more, but
one at the point of the street corner lot

where all summer I held my girl by the back
of her bike and ran the green block down.
The tree was obvious, catalpa, its long
three-branching trunks splayed like a birch, whose
shagbark white parchment skin is equally
unmistakable—leaves as big as a
piece of paper, if the page were a heart
or head of a spade, and pale green, foot-long-at-
least bean pods dangling like ropy toys—
three trunks pushing from our one earth, equally
thick, the same height. And then, among two trunks
of waving catalpa, I saw ash leaves, fist-
sized but delicate, blooming from the third.

    3.

All over the village the ashes are
dying. Already dead, my tree friend says.
The scourge emerald borer rode in on
shipping crates, Asia via Lake Erie,
2002. They date it to the month.
And in bundles of firewood, in luggage
of travelers, in bedding plants, their radiant
splay spread "like wildfire," up Ontario,
down, through Ohio, Illinois . . . and now
7.5 billion ash trees, mountain
white (fraxinus Americana) and blue,
fragrant, Carolina, green, (family of
Oleaceae), of opposite branching,
of compound pinnate leaf, whose timber is
"wonderfully springy," excellent for oars
and tools, "and lends itself to steaming and

4.

turning," as in bentwood furniture, will die.
Though some refer to them as trash. Trash ash.
What is a weed? And the answerer says
a plant that doesn't fit the local plan.
In my personal doctrine of signatures
you can tell the emerald ash borer
simply by its hole, the letter D, as
it emerges from the host—each circle
with its flattened edge or side—a hundred
or more, like buckshot, on a tree sometimes,
or on a tree braided to another tree.
Two catalpas growing with a third.
I pushed my daughter down the street, let go,
and her laughter lit the waiting trees—ash
or trash, catalpa, oak . . . the neighborhood
where she learned to fly. Then the trees grew wings.

FROM American Poetry Review

* * *

Thumb

Who means what it is to be human
and is scarred by childhood.

Thick and neckless. Your head shaped
like a gravestone.

A smile opens across the knuckle and disappears
every time you lift a tumbler of scotch.

Who holds a pen and lies.

Who holds a chopstick
in the language of still-twitching fish.

When you think of the past you form a fist
until a heart beats.

Once removed by a chisel. Then reattached.

You stiffen in the rain and dream
of pudding—a smooth, boneless lake.

Who butters morning toast
while wearing a butter hat.

*

Who fingers the ad for beef, grows numb
while talking to a girl on the phone.

Useless while typing. Useless
tool who only worships space.

A stump. A blackened stamp.
Your own private map of loneliness.

Who always leans to one side. Detached.
Distant from all others.

FROM CRAZYHORSE

* * *

Paraclete

Once, I was so patient.
Once, I was mousy and tender and I put out always.
Once, you ought to have seen me growing up in that teeny house
        with the five babies and
Mom just died and Dad thought Jesus came back to Earth in the
        year 70 AD.
Once, I had the cracking and busted-up hands of a poor farmer.
Once, I was a mother at the age of nine.

This is the period I will refer to as my "actual insanity." My
        "internment." My "lonelymaking."
Also known as my horrible secret, continent-wide.

You know that expression—all good things must be annihilated.
Well, lesions split up behind my ears like slugs inking their way
        toward my eyes.
I soon became blind. Blind and simultaneously

able to understand everything perfectly. I was the most intelligent
        person in Illinois,
and so it was with ease that I discovered I lived in a prison inside
        of a prison.

*

With the dawn of my intelligence, my husband (he's a lawyer, he
        examines land) called on
an alienist. The alienist asked me to empty my pockets.
I dramatically turned my pockets completely inside out.
What could I have? What have I ever had?

I had a little teeny tiny silver-plated bell in my breast pocket.

During my internment, I was as silent
        as: the crown molding, which was unpeeling.
        as: the land my husband examines—all that red peanutly dirt.
        as: kneading. And needing.

The alienist held out his hand expectantly.

I clutched the little bell until I felt its clapper slide against my
        palm—this I intuited as a request.
I clutched the little bell until it pulverized.

And the alienist—he—he—forcibly unclenched my fist, dumped
the powder into his drawstring pouch, and then—he—licked
between my fingers all the rest of that fine babyblue dust.

He insisted on looking me dead in the eyes while he was licking.

(He did not know that I identified as blind.)

But! I had another bell. An invisible bell that I saw in my mind
        and I could listen to it
just by blinking. When I slept, a clatter of angel hair wound itself
        around me.

When I slept, no one in the world would lick my fingers.

Pretend for a minute that you are me.

Pretend the papers have declared your husband to be a horse's ass.
Pretend your brother wrote The Bible: Part II.
Pretend your brother once chased you with an axe, and then
        murdered the president.

And by "the president" I mean the President.

For how many seconds could you remain contrite and
        hummingbirdlike?

And then please recall how I flitted around like a hummingbird
        for decades.
For roughly all my life.

This is why I was able to give my body up to that asylum. My body
        but not my mind.
You know the old saying—

Mind over your pasty waterlogged limbs.

Yes, they tried to drown it out of me.
Some new experimental "treatment"—

My feet were permanently pruned,
my ankles forever blue,
my body altogether hairless and stooping.

*

They say the lack of empathy is a dead-ringer for insanity. I have a
        new theory:

Too much empathy will singe a small hole, just barely noticeable
into your soul and each day you live your magnanimous life, the
        hole grows
and it grows until eventually it becomes a universe
and every piece of you sinks toward its bottom, which is a giant
        rusted drain
inexorably swallowing all of you. Your consciousness is last but it,
        too, slips through

and the only thing left is the one tear you saved, your final lament

for the state of the world, and when that dribbles out—truly, truly
you are left with nothing.

It will also ruin a marriage.

My most empathetic gesture was the day I walked those dirt floors
to your holding cell, my bouquet smiling up into your tired pink
        eyes:

nasturtium, gladiola, sunflowers, the dandelion heads

snapped off and floated up, a symbol of hope, some promise of
    brightness—

I've never been as tender as the day I asked you to end your life.

FROM NARRATIVE

{ 47 }

MICAH BATEMAN

* * *

O as Zero Sum (A Psalm)

End this, Lord. I said I said no.
You saw the O of my mouth
Surrounding the vowel,

Slurred fret of morning time in the slow stirring
Of my cereal O's.
See the O as spoon, Lord,

O as rounded spade—
Dig and feed Lord I open the O for sustenance
But nothing.

Have you seen how we advertise zeroness?
O is for zero calories.
O is for pitiful Onan.

O is the round of the long canal of the body
Down which zeroness flows and empties,
Lord it's like this,

We must get the jackal, chicken, and corn
Across the river. The river flows
But none will enter

*

Alive. Jackal takes chicken; chicken, corn.
What is left but entropy? River wins.
The boat scurries its course, emptied.

My father's father enters the boat.
My mother's mother enters the boat.
The boat is a cavity that cannot enclose

One tiny morsel. O energy.
This letter, Lord help us.
How can one graph a sound so empty?

Take a photo of the choir and trace the mouths.
I said no, I did. I said: Mandible,
No, I won't let you down.

FROM THE CHARITON REVIEW

JEFFREY BEAN

* * *

I Come from Indiana

I come from Indiana, where the only thing to eat
is clouds. I was born in a snowstorm, the blizzard of '78,
and like snow I come back every year, shaking my hair,
dancing to the slowest music, full of whole notes.
I come from Indiana, where the shoulders of the ground
grow hairy with grasses, where anthills swell up
into heat and the smell of tar shimmering over roofs.
I walk out wearing nothing but a huge coat of corn,
I vanish into the horizon but never leave, like a line
of highway traffic, I throw handfuls of myself into air,
the particles of me gather below streetlights like mayflies,
die in the afternoon then gather again, night after night.
I come from Indiana where faces grow plump in my dreams
like lettuce in soil and good men in towns pour oil
into mowers a few feet from wild deer, sniffing the wind,
hidden behind trees. I come from Indiana, where all the stories
about me are true: the day I stole that policeman's horse, the day
I drove my Honda blindfolded into a tornado,
the day I spray painted cellar door, cellar door
over and over on my girlfriend's cellar door until her father
chased me with a burning log into the woods, where
he couldn't find me because I was making love to his daughter
under a bridge in a thunderstorm. I come from Indiana,
and when I'm there I enter the air like a teenager

diving from a boat, the hard blade of his torso slicing the lake
while his mother, out of earshot, calls him home.

FROM *JUKED*

{ 51 }

JEFFREY BEAN

* * *

I Don't Live in the Kind of House

that in a pizza commercial would sell you pizzas.
For one thing you wouldn't like the colors of the walls,
and by you I mean you pizza lovers, dialing the numbers
on your phone right now, readying your tongue
to recite your list of toppings, and the problem with the colors
is that they're too dark for you, deep reds and deep blues,
and the wall sockets are plugged up with child-proof thingies
so my daughter doesn't stab in her finger and blow herself up,
my daughter who is incredibly sharp, she learned to clap
just by watching my wife clap, she brought her fingers together
and found a kind of safe electricity there that made her hungry.
She would have ordered a pizza if she could speak English,
she can almost say pizza but that doesn't cut it with Dominos,
what cuts it with them is money, crisp and folded, and you there
are now moving your money toward the hot cheese that zooms
at your doorbell in a car with brakes so bad even my daughter,
whose name is Olivia, who claps the way Chuck Berry plays guitar,
even she hears the sorrow in that metal scraping up to your door
past the brand new houses whose windows alone could sell you
a fucking triple-decker double-cheese goat meat pie with avocado.

FROM *CIMARRON REVIEW*

ROY BENTLEY

* * *

Saturday Afternoon at The Midland Theatre in Newark, Ohio

Slouched in a theater seat and watching Bullitt for the third time,
a look I get from an usher might best be described as granting
a general amnesty and full pardon for my having shelled out only
the one admission price. There's the balcony with its blue and red
curved seat backs. By a door to the upstairs men's room a framed
likeness of the Civil War drummer boy, Johnny Clem, whose baby-
faced looks and sudden-dark hair remind me of a young Italian,
then Sal Mineo in Rebel Without a Cause. There's that angels-
in-thearchitecture grand gesture of a ceiling, the wall of drapes
of eloquently pleated purple. And there's the screen framed in
its filigree of gold and silver. The usher is accommodating me
by simply not noticing—I'm on my third popcorn, third enormous
Coca-Cola, second box of Milk Duds, when I realize I'm happy.
Elated. In Ohio at fourteen you're disappointed most of the time.
So I want to tell Frank Bullitt just how it feels to be from Dayton
and new here, a fat-kid eighth grader at Fulton Middle School.
But then, Steve McQueen is French-kissing Jacqueline Bisset
good-morning. Strapping on a shoulder holster and .38 pistol.
Now he's stopped at the corner of Clay and Taylor, searching
the pockets of his trench coat/suit coat for change. I've loved
that look all afternoon. The usher reacts as if that says it, that
fuck-the-world expression of Frank Bullitt as he gives up and
bangs the cover and steals a newspaper. Turns out, 1968 isn't

for the faint of heart. You need a Mustang GT 390. Ice water
for a blood type. A tolerance for the visages of the dead you
made dead, slaughtering out of that old American purity of
motive that dissolves into a communion of terrific car chases
wherein thunderous algorithms of horsepower rule.

{ 54 }

FROM *THE SOUTHERN REVIEW*

MONICA BERLIN & BETH MARZONI

* * *

Begin not with coastline, not with harbor or cove. Begin

not with sea. No mast & no rigging.

No crow's nest, but crows.
So, begin with bevy & gaggle—

terms of venery, those nouns
of assembly crowding—with building

& cast & murder & brood, bouquet when flushed
from shaggy underbrush that startles

at the periphery, a collective flooding
then swallowed by sky. Begin not with sky.

Begin not with flood. Begin
underfoot the boy made of sand, beach

spilled out, almost promise, not moonlit &
not dawn, & off the shoulder. On the back

-road that slows us to breaking for the muted, for the rest
called backbone & broke-back, call breadbasket, call

*

heart-land, take back hard-pressed
& half-blood & downturn & dumb-luck. Take back

subprime & subsidized. Take back what slammed
loud out the door or whimpers in a corner

of a lean-to too far leaning. Words we'd have
to soap. When those wings beat hard against air

to take flight, why shake fists? Where
those birds dress branches winter strips, soon

the trees will be gone. We'll bow our heads,
look elsewhere. So, sure, there's no ocean

-made horizon, no shore to trace worn-down
edges we could find in any light. If each

curve was just cut by weather, its own
fierce moods, why pretend we've straightened out

& shored up. We can't keep any place
in its place. Some days the sky darkened with

wings can't shake the call, stop the pull
back, that tug against the distance

that's threatening to widen. & in that gap
where echo calls back & then away

{ 56 }

*

we pretend we can tell even the birds
how to live. We pretend by the rooftops,

the low swing of dusk. We scatter. We pretend
living among them is so hard

it becomes its own season. That the birds
make their own weather. & maybe so, & So, let's

begin in a maybe, not shutter up. What if
half-dim meant nostalgia turned quiet

hum in the mouth on the other end of the line,
or against the shoulder, longing not static

in the bridge between here & every day, swept up
& then? Maybe birds. Begin

every where the sky is &
the sky will not stop coming to winter.

FROM New Orleans Review

JENNIFER JACKSON BERRY

* * *

A Story of Girls

We stopped short of kissing, never
even practicing on fists in front of each other.
At sleepovers, we'd take turns:
Sarah, the flat one, never liked showing,
and I had adopted the quick flash,
whipping up my shirt after a 1-2-3 warning / look at me.
I had no idea the Kama Sutra describes seventeen
types of kisses. I thought the only variable for good
sex was bare flesh, that so much depended on nudity.
One afternoon behind Nicole's house
we pulled our shorts down around our ankles.
We planned to pull them back up
at the edge of the woods when her house was in sight.
We heard dirt bikes, the other fifth graders, the boys
out doing what we thought they did
on summer afternoons, racing, chasing squirrels.
Not before or since have I dressed so quickly.

I would soon realize the boys knew
even more than we did. I knew Amy
wore her day-of-the-week panties on the wrong days.
I knew Nicole saw one of the boys' things
after she was caught in a rousing game of Boys Chase Girls.
I had jelly bracelets winding up only one wrist

because I knew any adornment on my left meant
I was available—bit of wisdom from my mother.
My hair was long and curly, sometimes still in dueling braids,
even though I knew they weren't cool.
I hoped the boys would keep grabbing my hair
like handlebars. It would be years before I truly understood
anything about anything from behind.

Daughters of our own will learn sex
from their own generation of girls, no matter
how hard we try as mothers.
Our circle disintegrated,
but I heard, because girls always heard,
some of them were going down
on first dates. It had become tighter jeans, darker panties.
Tube tops, the first clue there were such things as sex clothes.
I stopped tonguing my fingers apart, stopped practicing
the pucker, then open. It had become real.
It had become gold bracelets and hair straight
as the arrows we drew through doodled hearts.

FROM The Chaffey Review

JASON BREDLE

* * *

Roman Candle

I want to rescue my neighbor's dog
from a field of roman candles
and I want to be naked when I do it
and I want to leap from a van
during my approach
and run with the dog in my arms
and the blackest of skies
over my head
and I want the dog
to be a Labrador retriever
and I want it to feel
like those nights in Berlin last fall
and I want it to feel
like the stars are crushing my skull
and I want to feel like I can resist
any type of pain
and I want to feel like I'm afraid
of absolutely nothing
and I want to feel like I'm in touch
with everything I see
and I want to feel loved
the way I love
everyone I meet
and I want to feel like I live

exactly the way I want
and I want to feel
prepared for the day I lose my tongue
in the Spanish zoo and I'm covered
with blood and have no one
to turn to and my friends have left me
to die alone in this unfamiliar church.

FROM FORKLIFT, OHIO

RICHARD CECIL

* * *

One Hundredth Anniversary Edition of "Birches"

Ice shouldn't look so pretty hung from trees
whose limbs are going to fall on power lines
and cut me off from light and heat for days.
Ice ought to be as black and dull as asphalt,
smearing what it clings to like spilt oil.
It shouldn't hang from sagging wires like tinsel
cheering up the dreary winter landscape
six weeks after Christmas. Sidewalk ice
should not look like a gleaming coat of varnish
brushed on to brighten up the dull gray concrete.
Ice shouldn't turn my neighbor's rusty Olds
into a fairy coach encased in glass.
If ice were only beautiful and useless
as ballet is, as poetry once was,
I'd praise it as the only luxury
that people with no money could afford.
No half weeks pay's required to see this ice show.
All seats are free, with equally good views—
though I prefer my city-country view,
where Frost-like glittering maples fill one window
while iced up streets and sidewalks fill the other.
Subtract a hundred years and I'd be thrilled
to jot down notes for "Birches" by my wood stove

with pen and paper lit with oil lamp light.
But, like a deep sea diver, I'm attached
by life lines that supply me all my needs,
even letters—pixels on a screen
that will go blank when my electric's cut.
(Which will be soon—my lights are flickering.)
When those wires snap I'll shiver in the dark,
cursing beauty that I ought to praise
in blank verse lines so eloquent that they're archived
in the 22nd century Norton On-Line Anthology.
But somewhere in my desk drawer there's a Bic
with ink enough to write a page or two,
before sun sets, of this mixed review
of Nature's Ice Show—a literal smash hit
as cars out front slide through the intersection
and branches out back shatter on the ice crust.

from River Styx

GEORGE DAVID CLARK

* * *

Python in a Grand Piano

Beneath the gloss
of lacquered walnut,
golds and olives
jigsaw. Muscle
and musk. Dust motes
in suspension.
Lengths of leaf-
and loam-colored
scales in wreaths
above the soundboard
like music at rest.
How a trailing silence
sometimes tricks us
into thinking
that a tune's released
its cincture on
the room. We fold
the sheets of Chopin,
see them vanish
in the bench. But
quiet doesn't
free us. Something
rasps and gathers
in the dark parts

of an open ear:
reticulated thunder,
yard on yard
melodic rope.
The score, we find,
is longer than
it seems and stronger.
To catch the thing
that knots us we
sit down and bait
the keys. Relax
and watch the parlor
grand digest
the small white mice
that were our hands.

FROM Narrative

SARAH COURY

* * *

The Girls

The Devil turned the water white
under the smothering heat of dawn

cockroaches twisted belly-up
swept out the back screen door

and mamas hid babies in pantry drawers
with a sack of salt and a crucifix

The Devil lay low in the cool soft clay
at the bottom of the sinkhole pond

where moss hangs like a woman's hair
from old tupelos that sing like a banished choir

in the rising white steam
when the hot rain falls

Set adrift in the scent of flowering dogwood
so thick it pulled them to the ground

girls made love to the boys in the cool soft clay
on the darkened banks of the sinkhole pond

*

while mamas slaughtered hens that were turning in circles
under hives the hornets left

The Devil arrived in a rush of white water
and mites ate the howling dogs

The girls huddled in caves that gaped from their ribs
opening after love

pollen of the flowering dogwood like scattered diamonds
fossilized on their tongues

at the bottom of the sinkhole pond
in the cool soft clay that never ends

where they lost their footing again and again
and fell together deeper and deeper.

FROM EMERGE LITERARY JOURNAL

CATIE CRABTREE

* * *

Self-portrait as the Futurist Manifesto of Women's Fashion

i   Machine-gun woman

Machine-gun woman will never be touched as a child or asked to touch
because everyone knows the Machine-gun woman becomes too hot for
        the human hand and
there is no easy way around the swivel rounds.

Machine-gun woman's long silvery legs she has three of them.

Machine-gun woman quick-change artist forces cover.

takka takka takka takka takka takka

Machine-gun woman says. Out of practice
                —what is this?—

Machine-gun woman is no Machine-gun Kelly no World War hell nor
        heroine but her dress
a suggestion of metal curve, a trigger peninsula suitable an army of
        lightning. You cannot
hold her, no, cannot shift to her Commodore swing.

takka takka takka she says,
and then her belt-fed, smokeless recoil.

ii   Airplane woman

wanders in air, heavier than air, fools gravity so as not to become a
smoking hole in the ground.

Her forward motion generates lift as the wing moves through space,
        zigzag décolleté
a sonorous, loud, deadly, and explosive attire.

Airplane woman is a Ramjet, a Scramjet, a spy satellite. Airplane woman
says hey, sky, and needs no one on board to glide. She forces air into
one side of her engine, and it ignites. Hotter and faster then, she looks
toward her attitude indicator, turn coordinator, vertical speed indicator,
horizontal situation indicator.

Airplane woman likes the wind to blow enough to ring the bells, catch
        the flag.

    Paper, cardboard, glass, tinfoil, aluminum;   ceramic, rubber,
        fish skin, burlap, gas;

    growing plants and living animals make up the Airplane woman.

Airplane woman is a wing walker. Only when she knows what's below
        her can she fly.
Airplane woman says look it's a bird. Airplane woman says biscuits and
        gravy, gravity and flight.

iii   Radio-telegraph antenna woman

There is no statute of limitations regarding indecent sexual assault to the Radio-telegraph antenna woman.

Athough she may look delicate, the four-year-old futurist Radio-telegraph antenna woman does not need to march herself down to the small town (small but long town) police department at the time of the event, nor does she only have until eight years of age to do so.

She is only four, five, six, seven, almost eight, and yes although she walks many places with her three brothers and one sister (her younger brother only two at the time of the event and right next to her, his antenna sparking slightly as well) and sometimes on her own, blocks and blocks of cement tee-peed over tree roots, she will not need to do this.

She is a real, living three-dimensional complex, and a small one for her age, often mistaken for a boy Dorothy Hamilling her way to school and at home, watching shampoo bubbles rise as she turns the bottle over and over again.

She looks herself up in her family's set of encyclopedias and learns that she has her own language. She is not surprised by this, nor that this language is necessary for accurate, rapid and secure communications. This sort of communication has not been available between Radio-telegraph antenna woman and her family. Radio-telegraph antenna woman has been known to pick up and record random noise, but that has never bothered her.

Radio-telegraph antenna woman may seem complicated, but she is really quite simple in her frenzy of spirals and triangles, speed and novelty, lights and clicks.

iv.   Submarine woman

This is how the Submarine woman can dive and then surface:

The heavy hollow boat loses weight in the sea.

```
                          | |             |||                    —————
Air tank     |    |     |   |   |      |    |   | |————
——————  / |ooooooooooooooo|           \ /  ——————
———-                \ \ |wwwwwwwwwwwwwwww|                     /
————————-X————-|———| |             | ———————-Ballast Tank
————————-Valve
```

Fill the ballast tank with water—the Submarine woman will sink.

Fill the ballast tank with air—the Submarine woman will rise, a silent
    sleeper.

    ——Yesterday a Russian mini-submarine sank after its propeller
        was entangled in fishing net.

    ——Bodies not wearing cement shoes float under ordinary
        circumstances.
    ——However, world record holders and seekers for free diving
        pass the point of neutral buoyancy and must actively swim
        upward, or they will sink.

Submarine woman is an evolution of the diving bell.

Submarine woman does not believe mangoes to be a "bedroom fruit."

*

This is how the Submarine woman remains:

The induction coil transformer, the source of electromotive force.

The courage.   The condenser.

The discharger, the spark balls, the quenching inductances.
The female equivalent of futurism. The leaping over vertiginous jaws.

Submarine woman dives and surfaces, sinks and lifts.

FROM THE LAUREL REVIEW

KAREN CRAIGO

* * *

Milk

Last night, a baby cried
outside my window and I knew
I should be holding it.
I was pretty sure
she was talking to me, my own baby
a thousand miles away,
grown hazy, not as clear
as the music from the courtyard.
I brought the hand pump
in my backpack and it took all day
to draw an ounce.
My baby and I are near the end.
It's no one's fault—each day
I have less to give,
less milk, I mean.
There's a magnet in me—
it's just a metaphor, so it's OK
that the pull is stronger
over distance. Let me return
to that baby in the courtyard,
to its terrible music
and how I wanted to go
to her, give to her.
And I cried a little, the way

mothers cry, and catch it,
and place it in smallest mouths,
so this morning there was a glass of it,
of milk—what the body repels
as it pulls the other to us.
The world is dense with hunger.
Sometimes I have to pull his fist
from my baby's mouth
just to feed him,
and I am mindful that hunger for some
is a fist that never stops
being a fist. What I'm trying to say
is I couldn't dump that milk.
For the baby in the courtyard,
for my baby, for all
the babies, I drank it down.

FROM ATTICUS REVIEW

CALEB CURTISS

* * *

A Taxonomy of the Space between Us

(0)

        The space between me and my brother
has always varied in size and volume (1):
               its dimensions
       are ever-changing (2),
  have bent and expanded,
     transcended literal confines (6),
           opened new spaces (3),
  abstract spaces (4),
       have functioned
          as a membrane (5)
  that wraps itself around our bodies
       like the well-tailored clothing
  worn in the 1950's (7)
       without ever actually touching us (8),
  connecting us without being (9),
          its existence
  predicated upon the fact that we still are (10),
and will remain being
      as long as one of us
         is still alive.

(1) This is a poem about me and my brother; about how the space between us is neither division nor connection. This is an poem about how time moves faster than our ability to perceive of it, and also, other abstract concepts that describe the space between two or more people as being both unknowable and exceedingly relevant. This is an essay about how memories are disorganized, about the longing I have for my brother and my sister and my sister who is dead.

(2) Shortly after he moved from our hometown in Champaign, Illinois to his new home in Salt Lake City, Utah, I travelled out to visit my wife's parents in Pennsylvania where I tried to write about a memory I have of watching the film Robocop (the mid-80s future-noir about a vigilante cyborg who violently exacts revenge upon a multinational conglomerate responsible for destroying the person he once was) with my brother (a). We were at a friend's house, and it was very late at night. My brother was no older than 6 and it was the first time he'd witnessed the wanton destruction of human life on a television screen, and so he was petrified, but would not stop watching, would not stop uncovering his eyes. It was not the furthest apart we'd ever been from one another.

    (a) I have searched my hard drive extensively for remnants of this writing but it's gone like the snippets of photographs my mother cropped away with craft scissors to focus on whatever object she wished to focus on: a house, a tree, a face, a body.

        (i.) I have come across these pictures here and there over the years. Oftentimes, all she's cut away is just a stack of magazines, or a table full of dirty dishes, a hand sitting on an arm rest: negative space

deemed unworthy, discarded, or mistakenly left
behind in a pile of photos like a glimpse into the
future.

(3)   It is hard to know for sure if I was closer to my brother when
holding his infant body down and punching him in his stomach,
or when gliding a pair of clippers over his scalp when he was in
the 7th grade, making him the first kid in middle school with a
Mohawk.

(4)   When I was 13 my brother found me next to my bedroom
window smoking a Camel Straight I'd bummed off of a man at
an AA meeting I'd attended with the intent purpose of finding
someone who'd bum me a cigarette (a). My brother promised he
wouldn't tell our parents and he did not and he has not. My brother
promised me that he would never start smoking and then he
started a few months later when his friend stole a pack of Marlboro
Reds from his dad. He still smokes to this day even though I quit 7
years ago.

(a)   It is true, various media sources have told us,
that children who are raised by smokers are more likely to
start smoking themselves. When I started I was 11 years old.
When my brother started, he was 12. Neither of our parents
smoke and so when they found out about our habit, they
did not understand how it fit into God's plan and so they
prayed over us in tongues, letting phoneme after phoneme
overlap with one another until they washed over us in
an ever-familiar haze.

(5)   Shortly after my sister died, my brother got a speeding ticket
and so I got drunk and I called him and I told him about how his

choice had disappointed me. He was living in Springfield, Illinois at the time and I was still in Champaign (I am still in Champaign). It was not the furthest apart we'd ever been from one another.

(6) My brother was talking about String Theory (a) before high school. About the multiverse: how the many universes that make up all of existence do not come into contact with one another just as the molecular vibrations that enshroud every object we touch in fact keep us from touching it, how our outsides coil around each other, affect each other without ever making contact, like the air that becomes entwined inside two separate balloon animals (b).

> (a)   According to my father, at some very elaborate point, any scientific theory can become so complex it can only be understood through metaphor and abstract association. This, of course, leads to a very strange ontology, as the referents for these metaphors themselves become more and more abstract so that, in the end, a perfectly rational person can find himself arguing for the necessity of faith, the existence of God and the presence of some unknowable reality governed by forces that transcend our understanding of time, space, and the nature of existence…

> (b)   There are numerous instances wherein both Art and Science agree that two objects can press up against one another without ever touching. Think Michelangelo: how Adam's outstretched hand nearly meets that of his maker. Think of Michelangelos's fingerprints: thousands of them embedded in that ceiling, as if you could actually touch what he touched.

(7)   I have dreamt that my brother is the one who dies, leaving me and my two sisters (one older, one younger) to mourn him for the rest of our lives. It is a strange relief to fall into. Stranger still to wake up in.

(8)   I have the cashmere coat that my great grandfather, Charles Dwight Curtiss I (a) (b) wore when he worked in Washington D.C. designing the interstate system that my brother and I once used to drive across country. It was the first time we'd spent that much time together after our older sister died on a country road when she missed a stop sign in what I sometimes imagine was a successful suicide attempt and other times imagine was a mistake. The coat is too big for me and too small for my brother. I keep it in my closet where it's slowly consumed by moths, a fact I pretend not to know.

(a)   (who begat Proctor & Gamble executive, Charles Dwight Curtiss II, who begat Water Chemist, Charles Dwight Curtiss III, who begat my brother and my sisters and me)

(b)   Shortly after I was born, my great-grandfather visited me in the hospital. At that point, my brain was a mass of unpaved passageways, my body a collection of cells which have all since been replaced with new cells. A few months later, he died, and his body didn't matter anymore.

(9)   Both my brother and I have spent our fair share of time shaking on church carpets, convinced of our bodies' inability to function as a conduit for God's everlasting love. I do not fully understand how this has affected him, nor do I know if he is an atheist like me. It has been some time since we've discussed spirituality, a fact attributable to our need to prioritize in all of the space that now separates us.

(10)   The first time our younger sister tried to talk to me about how our older sister was gone and was never coming back because she was dead, I referred her to my brother and went back to carving out a hole in time which has, over the years, become both a bivouac and an alter to what does and does not exist between me and my siblings. I have since become much better at leaving that space when the occasion calls for it, at visiting them for longer and longer periods of time. I have since become increasingly aware of what it means to be close to someone, to be far far away from someone.

FROM PANK

PAT DANEMAN

* * *

Polly's Mother Sang Opera

We heard her, never saw her—
voice like liquid in a glass, ice
crackling, cold condensing
on its curves as it slipped
through our fingers. We imagined
what we did not see—
black curls, lace dress, her face
a sad older version of Polly's.

Though what did older mean to us?
When you are 16 there is no other age,
no other way to look than tempting,
from the pink on your lips to the space
that opens when you spread your legs,
tan all the way into your underpants.

As for the real woman, who could say
if she was ugly or more beautiful
than her daughter, or if there was a bottle
on the bedside table? No one was allowed
in Polly's house, even best friends
got no farther than the front porch—
Polly leaning out, lifting her heavy hair,

*

from above, the flood
of music, dark forest
of words we did not understand.
At home our own mothers
ironing, sleeping, smoking,
while we stood at Polly's door
not knowing what we were
waiting for.

FROM MOON CITY REVIEW

STEVE DAVENPORT

* * *

Dear Last Nerve

I saw you at the liquor store yesterday not one hour after we rubbed fenders in the library parking lot and fussed all the way into Periodicals, where we made out like sticky magazines. You get around.

I admit my heart is wormy and I am downwardly mobile. Admit your sails are made of cheesecloth and your relationships end where they start. Let's fight.

I'll be your swizzle stick if you'll be my flight of martinis. Insert Another Quarter. We Are Nearing The End. Doorknob, Dead as.

I had a lover once who milked the last bit of me into a casing no thicker than a glance and fired it at me as I got out of bed to open my email.

I lost words for exit and re-enter. I have a hole in my bucket. I should keep my enemies close.

I hate you. Faithfulness is overrated. Marry me.

FROM New Letters

Emily Dickinson

She's all, like, "I like writing" and
"I'm good at it." She's, like,
"I like white and looking out
of windows," and, like, "I like
baking bread and the Bible," and, like,
"I like my alone time."
She's like, "It's cool."
They're like, "I don't know if it's cool."
She's like, "It is."
They're like, "You're weird."
And she's like, "No, I'm not. Maybe
you're weird."
And they're like, "No, you're weird."
And she's like, "Am not."
And they're like, "Are too."
And she's like, "na-uh."
And they're like, "uh-huh."
And she's like "Whatever!"
And "Talk to the hand!" And
"Whatever." And
they're like "Whatever."
and she's like, "Whatever."

FROM *TINA* (BLOOF BOOKS)

PETER DAVIS

* * *

Mother's Day

I feel my best when I'm on a skateboard.
On a skateboard,
I am another human, one more mobile
and more attached to a small plank of wood
set atop four small wheels.
My wife is very beautiful, Tina.
Physically it's like she is trying to eclipse
her inner goodness.
It's like she has decided to grow
a force field around her inner goodness
by creating a shell of beauty
that no one would dare penetrate. I have
penetrated this shell and am lucky.
Tina, I have been lucky
to be inside my wife
and watch my kids expand her belly
and see her explode with them.
She is not a skateboard but I am
free when I am sailing on her.
I look at her and the sea waits.
My ollie, sometimes, is
perfect, Tina. When it is, she snaps into the air

and when I land
my feet are just glued.

FROM *TINA* (BLOOF BOOKS)

KWAME DAWES

* * *

Just Play the Damned Tune

Journeyman, he knows all the tricks,
how to make room inside the crowded
belly of a tune for a surprise to wake up
to cause that stirring inside his head,
giving him ideas he could turn into
a surprise, get a hold of him. He knows
how to make space for the talent;
the world has rules. He knows how
to sit back, humble himself, draw
light away from him so the surprise
can happen. Journeyman will read
the contract and the rider, will
step outside and look on the marquee
to see whose name is out there,
and when they come, hours
into the rehearsal, and they start
to sing and play, Journeyman knows
to wait for a sound to break out,
before he settles himself into
the music. The talent might just
be an untalented fool, but if his
name is on the paper, then
journeyman knows to make
this talent sound like music.

He knows how to make a bed
for the horn to blow in,
and this sweet bed of sound
is the bedrock, the unostentatious,
unvarnished truth, and journeyman
knows to just play the piece,
let it be what it is so the talent
can find a place to shine. Journeyman
will always say the talent hit it
out of the park; journeyman is
going to be lying about this
all the time because journeyman
only cares about the cash in hand.
This is how the ordinary man
takes on the world, quietly,
simply, and journeyman is mastering
how to stand invisibly day and night
so that he can live long. Journeyman
will never know what surprises
he has in him, Journeyman will only
know what is outside himself;
that is the way his world must work.

FROM 32 Poems

REBECCA DUNHAM

* * *

Melancholia as Invasive Species

                as bloodroot,
bundled vascular and impervious

to the trowel, to the chemical
bath, to the plastic

pulled over it in sheets—
        it will not be expelled.

I close my eyes. The rotary tiller's
engine is a shell held to the ear,

its hot breath an insistent
sussuration: persist, persist

Not beauty. Not the milkweed's
orbed catch of petals but

jeweled pestilence, ravaging need
—its strange and sudden

*

      promise: hard
rain of black amid the grass,

fistful after fistful of wedding rice.

FROM *MERIDIAN*

KATHY FAGAN

* * *

Suburban Canticle

With your beard full of mice and a mouth full of hymns you sang
    for them.
Wearing offal perfume, all five wounds seeping and your blind
    eyes tearing
  in the sun, Francesco, you sang.
Iconic now, you are everyone's neighbor, spotted with birdlime among
    the mounds of daylilies that crack out
    their embers each day after trash day in the middle of June.

Crayolas crushed on the sidewalk are named Caribbean Turquoise
    and Sunflower Gold;
I didn't have to read their paper wrappers to know this.
I didn't toss in the dryer sheet or lay down the mulch around
    here either,
  but these are our top and our bottom notes now.

The Global Fellowship of Future Saints run in soccer socks on
    razor scooters.
Fireflies light the night for you, saith the Lord, and you shall have
    dominion
over all the creatures you spy with your little eye as you lie
  on your back watching clouds float by.

We're alike, Francesco.

I too was a child among gas mowers, picking warm tar from my
     foot soles.
The blades of the rotary fan reflected my days like a flipbook.
I was devout for such a long time, but wore my summer clothes and
     walked
   barefoot on the bees and their clover so briefly.

Because you reside beside them in heaven now,
you know that Anne Sexton pastes firecrackers into her scrapbook,
that Joseph Cornell hoards fan magazines.
That's like us, too, Francesco:
   metaphorical yet concrete.

Let me be clear:
   If I pray to you on my knees under the sycamore, I am asking you
     to let us stay.
Like the honeysuckle, we love it here. We don't care who we crowd out.

FROM NINTH LETTER

RICHARD FOX

* * *

Explaining Pictures to a Dead Hare

after Joseph Beuys

Human labor—
human error—
like Jack or Jill:
what goes up
must come down.

Hill as sine wave;
has peaks & valleys.

Here is Jack.
Here is Jill.
Here are woods.

Here is stream
& well.

Here is hole
for rabbit—
hare & Jack
(in tumble)
come before Jill.

*

Sky-parts fall
& here comes hare
from his eye-like hole
on fur-lucky legs—
his leap; his pin-up;
his wife-beater
& his amazing slacks.

FROM BlazeVOX

MARC FRAZIER

* * *

What Lies Hidden

When you felt abandoned,
I had not abandoned you.

I dreamed a memory:

in the rushes
gently rocking,
        the insects' hum—
a lullaby,
a reminding.

*

How were you saved?
Among so many.

When did you become
one drawn from the water?

The river speaks of many things,
including
how a mother's hands do what is needed:

the weaving of rushes,

the sealing with pitch.

How even a great soul cries for her warmth.

How we cry for freedom.

*

The beginning of many voices.
My own.

Even hers:
I pulled him out of the water.

Meaning
I had him pulled out of the water.

A slave is not born.

A mother knows which child's hands will do great things.

The Nile is only the beginning.

FROM EVANSVILLE REVIEW

STEPHEN FRECH

* * *

Enough, Not Enough

i.

How difficult it is to be simple,
to see a river and not ask where it runs.

How difficult not to think of friends' voices
in the gossip of river and stones.

How difficult to hear geese overhead in late winter
and not imagine in their cries the questions Where? How far?

not envy the earliest sign of spring aching in their bones.

ii.

The current hurtles downriver to blind rooms.
The recurrent water of the eddy doubles back,
healing itself, waking.

We swam at night
to the boulder in the fast current,
one by one taking turns,
guiding each other through the dark
with our voices.

*

For the swimmer,
the moon is untouchable,
elusive on the water.
For the one on shore
guiding him, he swims across the moon,
swims the moon's darknesses.

The shattered pieces of light
reassemble on the current.

iii.

The line between the current and recurrent
trembles, fraught with whirlpools;
our bodies like dropped sticks
crossed and recrossed, pulled under
and resurfaced almost untouched.

The stone's waist worn and narrowed
at the waterline, its warmth above,
the slick algae below,
the tug of the eddy
pressing against the stone.

What moves beneath,
what passes around us?

All that time, the boulder yielding,
losing itself, worn to pieces,
passing bit by bit on the lichen breeze
all over my body.

iv.

The fatigue I feel halfway across the distance,
my feet dangling into cooler water,
the moon on a smooth, passing surface;

friends silent now, gone, or missing,
carried on a current,
almost out of reach:

you fear that you are empty.
Still, there is a you that travels well
on rough seas,
pressing into and parting the water
of your own reflection,
a skin boat sailing toward luck.

v.

Because we cannot know,
because the future has a way of inviting itself,
the shipwright weighs the live and dead loads,
buoyancy and displacements,
support intervals,

beams of varying thickness and weight.
The bottom of the boat we ride to deep water,
pitched like a roof—
let the seams be true.

*

We dissolve on the water like snow,
light leaking through the water that is my body
and the water that is not,

enough, not enough
and the skin in between.

FROM NINTH LETTER

JOHN GALLAHER

* * *

In a Landscape: XIII

How many people haven't you married, that you thought
for a moment—who knows—maybe you would? It seems to me
right now that one should take such things
as warnings, but of exactly what, I'm not sure. We should all
be allowed to feel this near miss, how many things happen
at the same time, and how people have varying degrees
of perceiving that. That could be the warning. Or just
that "you never know." Or better, that line by Chuck Berry:
"It goes to show you never can tell." And so and so,
and so and so. But even with all the parsing, at some point
there will only be one person left. When my uncle died, for
instance,
he was playing cards with my aunt. It was his move
and she just thought he was thinking. If so,
he's been thinking a long time. When she died a few years later,
I don't know who was there. Someone she loved,
I hope. And if not that, at least someone.

I hit a possum once, late at night on my paper route,
1990. I stopped and looked back at it lying there
in the road—a patch of blood on its head. Then slowly
from the bushes past the curb, several more
possums appeared. They went to the one I hit. It
almost looked like a ceremony, light as a feather,

stiff as a board, or something. And the possum rose to its feet,
wobbling a bit, and followed them back into the bushes.

At some point that one thing will be for certain:
we're standing in line. I picture us there
as if at an airport waiting for our various flights
to be called. And from my spot in line, I worry
about the people around me, like when Natalie
was at her first sleep-over. Mostly I worry
that she'll be comfortable, and that she won't
feel lost. Eliot, who's three, was lost for a while
the other night. I was in the kitchen
reading John Cage's SILENCE, and he
was playing in the living room as the house
grew a little dark, and then I heard him call out,
"Hey guys. Hey, where did everybody go?"

FROM FIELD

BRANDI GEORGE

* * *

My Best Friend and Me

At ten, too old
  for dolls, we hide them.
 The toy bin snaps
   like a sacred book's
binding. While our parents
   sleep, we write ourselves
 gods, and the simple plot
   we began spins from us until
the characters start
   to question the rules of
 their universe; they do
   terrible things; they horrify
and excite us until morning.
   And I wish I
 could end here, but the dolls
   are already changing faces,
appearing in drawers. My mother's
   car doors are opening
 by themselves, and the house
   is cold, cold
as the halls between biology
   and gym. We fail
 our classes. Someone yells
   lesbians; the word spits

like the fire pit where
    my stepfather burns
  dolls, poems, stories thick
    with dialogue. He calls
the exorcist, whose business card
    was given to him by Pentecostal
ministers. These same men
    guide me through
a twelve-step recovery program
    for the possessed. I renounce
yoga. My parents
    divorce and we move
    to another town. My little cousin
dies, but I dream it first.

FROM *GULF COAST*

TYLER GOBBLE

* * *

A Natural American Spirit

Get off the internet. It's your birthday, America.
Tomorrow seems so frightening. With whom
fulfillment lies, rather the weight of it, the wait for it,

will S ever finish the eagle begun for you? Perplexing—
the spiritual is not first, but the natural, then the spiritual.
There is emotion in the two, things to be learned.

A charming young creature takes six instances
of caffeination and finally unrobes, then rerobes.
I've recently found myself inside a transplanted

heart. Instructions: Thomas Edison is buried here,
well, was. There is nothing natural about smoking,
except perhaps the feeling of being composed

of a wee bit of fire. Whitman and his haunches.
Whitman relies on the natural rhythms of speech,
on his innate ability to return the better pair

of pants to the young fella who needs them most.
This statement is directed at you. It'd like you to stop
and remember just why it's so possible for beautiful

men and women to fill the day. A masquerade of cities.
More pointed wires, like strings on a guitar
never lopped off. In order to save a few moments.

In order to snag the Hot Pocket directly when done.
In order to appear to care less about appearances.
In order to be eligible to receive special offers. The mail

arrived during the middle of this poem, as it does
in the middle of every poem. Mr. Gobble, you must
go on this once-in-a-lifetime horseback riding adventure.

Horses have such marvelous presence and sometimes
a poem, or piece of art, is able to capture some
essence of that presence. At the end of the journey

you'll find a campsite, tonight's fire already with bacon.
A woman will be there to take your photograph.
There is something natural about smoking, as is a concrete patio

by the river, hand-sewn bikinis and their lotion. One-time charges
for hair removal. Many of us have been witness to the experience
of fine dining. As a child, I couldn't leave my seat

until I cleared my plate, couldn't splash into the pool
for twenty minutes, couldn't even touch the basketball
until my mother was sure I'd digested. Now, the game is on

before I've even decided between the meatloaf
and the spaghetti for 9.99. America, what in God's name
have you done to my mid-section? Distraction with simple

*

facts: if the whiskey was made outside of the United States,
it cannot and never will be bourbon. If you are considering
an attempt to be rather strong for the rest of this year,

try a quest where you must restore the Curious Nature,
the Natural History, the Nature Walks in the gooseflesh morning.
The gal does not hope I request photos of her naked.

She loves to be draped in exquisite designs and I have no confidence.
The last rumor I heard of myself, I had disabled my Facebook
and strolled into some forest in the Ukraine. At the beginning

of 1999 in Chernigov, metaphysical beings who inhabit
the city did some sort of magic ritual, but from here,
I can't be sure, nor should I make assumptions.

What country can preserve its liberties if its rulers are not
warned from time to time that their people preserve the spirit
of repetition? Occasionally, I like to fry up bacon and eggs for dinner.

FROM *SIXTH FINCH*

* * *

Son

At the supermarket a woman gasped.
She asked me to play her son
at her husband's funeral. Her boy was in prison.
She wanted acquaintances to see a full
family, vital and right. In the limo, Mom said,
"Now say tender things to me, and I say
tender things to you." At the coffin, Sister
made a shrieking sound. Mom toppled over.
Here I am Dad, I held his hand.
When asked to speak, the voice was not mine,
and I could finally say the obvious things:
"Daddy was a mountain. Tenderness
was not his nature, but I am not
a typical son. He was so funny when we were young."
As I spoke, Daughter leaned on my arm
(she looked too young to play along).
Then I sat with her before the mountain;
she watched me and pulled on my beard.
She said, "Let me ask you this, Papa. Where are you?"
After the funeral, a handful of mourners
stood at the road. Dad's buddy
from the war, eyes heavy, told me
there is nothing to fear. Wife put her face
in her hands. Her beauty pushed against me

from the depths of her best dress. I kissed her.
It was insane, as if I had just come into existence.
Then Mom said, "It costs me to look at you."

FROM NEW LETTERS

JUSTIN HAMM

* * *

A Real Team Effort

And here you'd gone and told yourself
the morning couldn't possibly
get any worse, not after you realized
you'd left your jock strap swinging
from your bedroom doorknob, as you rushed
headlong into the purple prairie morning, late
again for the six am travel bus
and facing the prospect of a doubleheader
behind the dish without proper protection.

And that's when you see it: your mother's
souped-up Camaro comes peeling
into the high school parking lot, skids
to an action-movie stop in front of the bus
just as the driver jerks her into drive,
and now, incredibly, here is your old man
sprinting in desperation, a thief or a madman,
and there is something in his right hand,
something which he has tucked against his side
for protection, as if it were a football
or perhaps an enormous jewel of untold value.

*

There comes a pounding and the driver
cranks open the side door with impatience,
and then he has your jock, which he has just
received from your panting, sweat-slicked pops,
and he—the driver—is holding it out away
from himself as if it might be radioactive,
and now he's turning, handing it delicately to Coach,
whose face goes cruel with wind sprints
as he turns and passes it off to Klein the freshy,
cursed to the front seats for having ears
too sensitive for upperclassman conversation,
and Klein the freshy hands off to Castillo
the backup catcher who's gunning for your job,
and Castillo with a snicker gives it to Rosenthal,
and Rosenthal—God help him—holds the thing
a second too long and lifts it toward his nose.

Then Martin, Berringer. Then Jonesy and Little Nick.
And so it goes, every man's hands on your jock strap
until it reaches that SOB Looney, two seats up,
Looney who could reach right out and hand it
to you himself, save you that final humiliation,
but instead he passes it to the team manager
who is sitting in the seat directly in front of yours
because she's beautiful and because you planned it that way.
Now she turns and there it is, dangling between you,
frayed and a little off-white from two years of use.
Through the straps you can see her eyes, two dark
lakes where so many other sensitive boys have gone
and gotten themselves thoroughly and finally drowned.

{ 111 }

*

You reach out to take what is yours, and you wonder:
is this what the old broken men think of when they stare
out their windows into empty backyards, swigging
their warm beers and sighing now and then?

FROM PUNCHNEL'S

DENNIS HINRICHSEN

* * *

Caravaggio's Medusa as a Box of Nails

Forty pounds of iron/brass/wood screws
lag bolts/nuts/picture wire
this was the aluminum milk box my father used
to keep his refuse hardware in
Home Town Dairy filled to the brim
I had to push it a corner at a time
twenty dollars at a time
to get it from under the bench
so I could palm its spiky crown
it was useless treasure to me
all the things a man never builds
solidified by gravity
to one nuclear core
more tomb debris than new circuits
drywall shimmering like panels of milk
a hundred times I set my hand down
to lift a portion of that writhing head
my gaze pushed into polished concrete
itself a mirror reflecting my twisted face
shoulder/mound of bicep
veined and pumped
who would turn to stone then
sister ratting another doll's head with match
and comb

mother singing to baby brother/baby blue
diaper pin
dangling from her mouth like a cigarette
neighbor kid in the next yard
with a tommy gun
doing his best Vic Morrow belly crawl
Vietnam
not even a cool silk jacket yet
a fading dragon tattoo
father finally down from the roof
punctured/ shingling
gone/and back/alone
shoulder sore from where they gave him the tetanus
six-pack under his arm
or just me
that handful of nails I managed to lift
like a possible future
little Gorgon's face reflected
in bubbled aluminum
her astonishment at her own terrifying glance
like the birth of death and bone
I held the package tight
in the damp spring air
brought it down like a reckless hammer
nail to nail/screw to screw
building something bloodied/muscled
then stepped across the threshold
and climbed high in the apple
(which you can do as a child)
as winged as Pegasus with blossom

FROM *THIRD COAST*

AMORAK HUEY

* * *

She Blinded Me with Molecular Nanotechnology

First thing in the morning, we're already
trying on hats, scrubbing away at smeared selves.
Size matters, but not the way you think it does.
Mirror steams. We finger-scrawl messages
in this fog, think ourselves original. I shave.
She showers and provides perspective:
a nanometer is the length my beard grows
in the time it takes to lift razor from sink to skin.
Even the smallest spot of blood holds all our secrets,
those lies I've told or thought or lived
staining this tear-away tissue against my neck,
the deaths I've beaten and the one I won't
enmeshed in that fragile twisted code:
think of the stories this blade could tell.
To answer questions before they are asked –
this is marriage, or science, or close enough. We think
we are permanent but that's only temporary.
Hurricane's coming. The ocean's a mess,
those who care already putting value to damage.
We are not insured against flood.
Someone launches invisible wires into the storm

to measure the strength of impossible,
the color of wind. The more we know
the more we know. If you can collect the wires after
you can rule the world. We collapse
into bed, we mouth and skin and savor
and pretend our touching has purpose.
We passive each other's aggressive
and call it communication. We are without
power for days, we are not alone,
we are still wobbly from last week's earthquake
which we never saw coming. Tomorrow
remains our blind spot but we're working on it.
Married four years and I still don't understand
what she does when she's somewhere else
or the way her mind moves even when she tells me
the key is finding atoms of similar size and stickiness.
This is the future. This is fiction.
This is the world's smallest electrical motor,
controlled by chemists at 450 degrees below zero,
rotating in a way that is not random. Hey,
it's something. It's vanishing point and given day
and the discovery that makes possible
a new kind of miracle. This is proper noun,
payday, pitfall. We need a special microscope
to talk to each other anymore. We're still trying
to replicate the subatomic sophistication
of a potato. We scan and tunnel
and every system leads to another until there is no
molecule we cannot create from scratch.
Ten years ago we thought we were ten years

from having enough tiny robots
to live happily ever after. Maybe
nothing has changed, maybe everything.
Imagine the heart that heals itself.

FROM The Cincinnatti Review

AMORAK HUEY

* * *

The Wikipedia Page "Clowns Who Commited Suicide" Has Been Deleted

There are community standards to uphold. Red rubber noses to thumb.
And so many questions about process. Do you remove

the humongous shoes before kicking away the chair? Wash away
white grease paint before placing muzzle to temple? What about wig,

polka-dot bow tie, oversized glasses? How many versions of yourself
fit into tiny car before you connect hose to tailpipe? Oh, I should not

make light of my own pain, except that's all I know how to do. Blame
my cartoon tears, the awkward orange light in this tent,

the decade I grew up in: all those packs of Marlboros
I bought for my mother while she idled

in a station wagon jammed with screaming siblings. Or the pot
my father grew along the back fence, the babysitters in hot pants,

The Joy of Sex on the bedside table. Those days
we would have bet the future looked like Pong,

all pixilation and promise and just enough danger to be interesting:
we rode across country standing up in the front seat

*

between squabbling parents, we were missiles
ready to be launched at slightest tap of brake or hint

of international incident. We knew staying safe
meant huddling on hallway carpet with hands on head

and holy shit, you should have seen that carpet—
ten years of brown and green and orange shag,

plus I'm not even going to talk about the wall-hangings,
just the word: wall-hangings, for Chrissakes. Tells you

all you need to know when an entire generation has been intimate
with macramé. You probably think I'm telling stories

now, that this would be better off as prose,
but let me tell you something real, and pay attention

because I don't do this often: every line breaks
somewhere. It's no wonder we grew up and gave

our children everything they asked for. It's no wonder
we say there's a pill for every ill and we don't trust our institutions,

though we're either lying or mistaken because we believe
everything we've ever read or heard or seen or swallowed:

kick center-pole from under tent one hundred times,
we still take it on faith when they say it won't happen again.

{ 119 }

*

It's no wonder we made a career out of this costume party:
say the word and we'll play the fool, provide the distraction

that enables someone else's sleight of hand, we'll carry
the ringmasters' top-hats. It's no surprise

our closing act falls short of significance.

FROM REAL: Regarding Arts & Letters

ROCHELLE HURT

* * *

Infants of the Field

"Stories of rescuers finding small children alive after
tornadoes have carted them off have become so common
as to seem apocryphal."
— Patrik Jonsson, *Christian Science Monitor*

The wind has wanted to keep you as promised things,
captured and slung from the trees like giftling skins

on the hunting rack in the yard, your fathers' animal
anger for all to see, a heap of sour evenings—

mothers trapped like starlings, wanting the world
through a window, thinking of how a creek behind a house

always looks cheap like cellophane with the knowledge
that it dries up a mile down. No one has loved you

like the earth in its lupine fits, its precious jaw, steel hinge
of wind, the vapor tongue, only wanting to raise you

by the necks from your mire of too-soft flesh,
miracle cubs, pawing at death. No one has swaddled you

tight enough to keep it out, but now the wind
wills its song from your paralytic mouths—

*

the catch-all caws of child-fright the neighbors hear
at night, mistaken in thinking you were gone.

They remember it into the throats of their dinners
the first time it took more than one bullet, the echo

rattling in the walls as dusk puckered into evening.
They sing along, layering their animal calls

into a bunting of sun-dried pelts, waving
over the morning when they find you in the grass, arms

gravel-scrubbed, cheeks rough as salt licks, tiny
rain clouds of warm breath still suspended above

your pied heads. Storm orphans, they make a home in you
who escaped the grip of your fathers' disappointment,

you who were spit back like words into the named world,
the chosen changelings, only a little death-bitten, only a little

wild, those snarl-cries like a hymn half-recognized.

FROM Crab Orchard Review

ROCHELLE HURT

* * *

Some Oz

for my father

We stand at the top of the Miamisburg Mound
overlooking the industrial district, a stacked complex

of glistening roofs and chain-link stapled onto the plains.
You want photos of the coming funnel clouds

as they birth themselves. You want to be close
enough to grab the tail of one like a bridle

and ride it into another life. You are dreaming
of *The Wizard of Oz* cyclone scene—the lunatic

chickens blind-weaving through dirt, the tumbleweed
limbs of uncles blowing into the cellar

as the mares bolt for one lick of life unsaddled
before the end, and the twister bends

like a finger in the distance, beckoning.
You are remembering how you envied their abandon

the day you watched your mother divide
her teeth into those inside and outside

her mouth, let the difference determine
how many counties away the next storm

would fly her from your father. But he beat her to it,
his cement-dipped boots left on the porch for years,

sequined with mill rust—your sad-pageant shrine,
reminder to wake into your life, lest you lost yourself

to the dream of a sparkling city, or a heart
still clanging inside a steel man.

I am thinking of a postcard you sent me
from the Aviation Museum: *You know how they flew*

those old planes? Big as boats, but it was all
in the slope—aerodynamics.

Carve yourself a wing from the shale of this place,
you wrote—something to fly you out

of the black basin of old age. You sent that one
from the road, our runaway, storm-chasing.

I'm embellishing again. Those postcards were never sent,
and you didn't have to travel to find disaster.

You just wanted to be alone with your ache.
I've been thinking it wasn't the rush

so much as your love for them—from the first time
you scooped the wind onto your tongue

and swallowed as much as your tiny body could hold:
that sweet smelling air that parents a stillness

you knew in the womb, the murky drown and dazzle
of debris among the astral billows, swimming

flecks of metal trailer roofs like confetti, the faceted glare
like an infant memory of the world before it settled

in your eyes. Even before you saw one, you dreamt
its hollow center, you said—a self you recognized.

You were mesmerized by its blind anger and promises
of change in the boot-scraped landscape

of western Ohio. Where else could it take you?
Almost a decade away—and you might have remained

on the ground only as a shadow in spin, dropping
the occasional postcard to us from that far funnel

you lived in, hoping to be tossed into some Oz,
where your sisters were all thin stalks

of beautiful skin, yet unhusked by men,
your father alive, your mother unbruised.

*

Some Oz where the clock of your life could unwind.
But you've returned to us now, your hands

full of years like salvage. And how could you
have known what you'd wake to—a home

inescapable, you wearing your father's face.
Here on the mound, I understand you

feel impossibly heavy, your mind a foundry of regrets
as you search for a word like an opening

into some storm strong enough to take us both
to a place where your daughters can forgive you.

FROM Crab Orchard Review

LIAM HYSJULIEN

* * *

On Learning of My Father's Illness

November 22, 2011

I don't believe in anything,
but nature-via-beauty-con-science—

no cable that welcomes us
all home.

The crafted shore
of crying birds.

Alone in the belly
of a single branched tree.

I find these things all with you.

Or the words we rearranged
and the combinations that split
along the dirty water in my head.

I like this soulless hum
of metallic drivers, pistons firing

into the atomized filaments that wrap
down into the base of your spine.

*

I like it all these days. The drive through the loosened

rocks of the Cumberland. The moments in

our silence, the dipping in and out of range,
a mesh of spidered and fallen trees.

The darkening sky, the opening of the universe

dancing in a beautiful comb of white across what

I am still remembering

even now.

FROM MAYDAY MAGAZINE

RICH IVES

* * *

A Picnic in Nebraska

Let's allow for the unacknowledged music. And horses
in the neighboring field perhaps. Suppose
a platter of orange peels remained on the blanket.
Suppose a dream of a miraculous pillar
of distant oyster cream had haunted
the groggy afternoon nap, the wine bottle

inviting bees in for a short wet walk. Suppose
the afternoon's symbolism wasn't wasted on you,
almost sublimely pleasant you suppose, but so quickly
over and therefore a truly superior
disappointment. And now
I can't seem to remember

what a pheasant looks like. Even the trees here
cluster together, dry and brown and correct in their uniforms,
standing tall and away from the dangerous few farmers
fully enclosed in their plexiglass cabs
who no longer seem to desire
the same things we do.

Couldn't we invite the folk stories,
even if the country's not ours? Perhaps a talking fish
or a mule hiding a stubborn treasure. Perhaps

another wooden bride. Even if her leaves
have got to stop, couldn't we fashion a sturdy axe handle
and offer a few more shares in the old soil bank?

The breeze is back, and a careful assortment of clouds.
Let's give the uncertain evening our full and temporary
attention. Let's try to accept the grain's promise.
Suppose this dirt sea furrowed the courtship. Suppose
homesteaders living under sod roofs had burrowed
beyond the reach of any future with you in it. Suppose

the abandoned gas pump and the dead diner. Suppose
another dog-eared blue neon motel under the reservoir,
the ceiling too deep to sprout. Then perhaps
you're not really from here and when you begin
once more circling my mouth, what I welcome
barely resembles this ocean's lost and ancient tattoo.

The neighbor's baby hound dog on the porch begins
practicing his something you want in the trees howl.
His complaint's answer is not an open door
or something dead falling but the echo of that other
voice across the dark hollow, just when you've
decided you're the only one chasing the mystery.

FROM Apple Valley Review

SEAN KARNS

* * *

From a Tree Limb

Outside my house, a gutted buck dangles
from a tree limb. Two men pull the buck's hide
like tugging on a bell rope in a tower.
Their children swing on the swing set.
I've never seen a deer slaughtered,
never seen many things slaughtered.

I once saw my father gut a squirrel.
Doesn't smell right, he said. He put the squirrel
an inch away from my face.
Sniff it, he said. I smelled it, sucked in the odor
like my last breath and shrugged my shoulders
not knowing what I was sniffing for.
He dug a hole in the yard.
You got to dig the hole deep enough,
he said. So the dogs can't smell it and dig it up.

I wonder where the heart is,
where the spleen is,
if the men will leave the buck
disemboweled in two locations.

*

I press my face to the screen door.
A child pets the hide splayed over
the laundry line, the other watches
the hacking off of hooves.

FROM *PLEIADES*

NATHAN KEMP

* * *

An Accidental Horse-Sighting

It takes a belief system   Berries before
ripening   Walking in the patch
where no one is allowed   Talking
about luck running out & my damned
teenaged tastes   O, what wondrous
ass   O, white light overhead while I talk
about oral sex with an agreeable stranger   Better
to speak frankly   My hypocritical nature
of taking haircuts for more than they are worth:
troublesome   I keep my eye on the blessing   Which is
warm & I cannot wait to get closer to you
No hotel will let us sleep   Our hands & mouths
are built to last   An accidental horse-sighting
is what they will call it   & we are off

FROM ILK

* * *

Genetic

1.
Ash-good-sharp-love

is the word for needle
the nurse says
in another client's language

this is for genetic testing
she says

sign here

2.
when we were little
we went swimming swimming
every day

a pond with deep green algae
a garden spilled with weeds

Caravaggio would have seen
the shadows I
saw only heat waves, humidity

a dog panting
an overblown pink rose

my shirt a t-shirt
my skin red
peeling down to white

3.
Now we live outside
DC NYC LA

a set of initials
is not a home

when our parents died
we had them cremated

we burnt the old house
to the ground

then like the old cowboy
story—we got up on
our high horse

& rode the other way

4.
My daughter's
school lets out

to crows chasing an owl
they are nothing to me—

loud caws
shit

unless they are ravens
they don't belong in any poem

I have my standards

Miss Wisconsin, my daughter says,
reading the flyer, What do
you bet her hair is blond?

5.
Behind the reader at one book store—
self-help books

at this one—literary criticism

Is anything implied here?

6.
as the plane went down
the paper said

it was quiet as a library—
a library hushed
as a falling plane
how many have of us
have fallen?

*

so quietly—so far

7.
Yes I had a father,
I tell the nurse

no he's not alive—
heart attack no history of cancer

A mother, dead too—
cancer

a sister—cancer—living still

grandfather, grandmother,
grandfather—cancer,
cancer, cancer

my father's mother?
he always said
she swam away

Ash-good-sharp-love

she sticks the needle
in my vein

8.
What can you say about
your life in

so little space?

*

What will your daughter's
daughter say?

FROM *DIODE*

JOSHUA KLEINBERG

* * *

Chapter Concerning the Baker Act

She read that you've got to pluck out the sinner:
the prejudicial eyes then gone from the skull,
serpents of optical nerve tied into
a stagnant ribbon over the nosebone,
like hi-fi wiring—thin and red, and yellow
and black. And somewhere, below
the cavernous sockets, the wiring stops,
rooted in something hard and sparkling,
a strap molasses black diamond of heat,
pulling from not where you'd think,
but clotted into a fist where the thighs
meet—right where the boys try to piss
their anodyne sadnesses into collectible
glassware, rendering daydrunk photo-
manipulations. The scenes occur to us now,
not as a movie like normal—with telegraphed
hitches and movement and stuff—
but a series of digital stills.
When I consider the change in lighting
from one remembered scene to a next,
I am horrified again about the frog
in the pot. When I curate my intentions
there's suddenly so much
of the witchy forest crackling in me:

a faction of deadness unleashed on a
stumbling dumb girl, hands breaking
up through the soil, a hunger
for the ankle, for polemicized shoulder,
your bad dancing on the rooftop, as you
take off your shirt. I for one,
am not much the party animal. I am only
a halcyon drunk, and you, my darling,
you're everywhere at once. I can't
begin to keep up. You might do
the banshee thing, when the bars
are still sleepy and empty.
You might put a brick through
the karaoke window, trench a back
with your blood-painted nails,
but they're only applause lines,
a marvelous display, rooted somewhere
in helping. Give me a tire iron
and all your 7th grade dreams.
Give a sick man a dime for some rye
and a heinous act without a rebuttal.
Let's see.

FROM H_NGM_N

* * *

Borges: They Are Knocking the Wind Out of Me in Iowa City

Up late, reading alone I saw how Minturno was fooled by the intricacies of beauty. Unfortunately at that hour there was no one to tell (as a friend once wrote:" Everyone I know is either dead or still asleep.")

"Don't talk to yourself" I told myself. "Don't scribble in the margins."

When Marsilio Ficino said that beauty was just shapes and sounds he was surely bathing outdoors.

Neo-Platonists ease their bodies into their warm baths. Close your eyes you can see Minturno bathing under the autumn stars.

& so I went to bed at last & dreamt of my first city—Helsinki, late fifties—the old man in the harbor selling potatoes from a dory. In the dream as in life that old man was wearing a red shirt, the first I ever saw.

Minturno: ideal forms are the source of our passionate failures.

The next morning I walked in the street and felt too many things to be judged a success.

*

A man on stilts was handing out fliers announcing the arrival of a circus. It was a French circus. The man was speaking French.

"Ah," he said in French, "you are blind."

He withdrew the flier and tottered away.

I resisted the impulse to shout after him in my high school French: "You sound like the first dull minute after a train wreck!"

The stilts made a metallic tic-toc on the paving stones.

"Tic-toc, train wreck," I said to myself, feeling my tongue dent the soft palate. That was my method of keeping silent. Tic toc…

FROM LETTERS TO BORGES

DANIEL LASSELL

* * *

We Have a Llama Whose Name Is "James and John Sons of Thunder"

My mom named him that because she's into the Bible. In fact, all our animals are named after biblical characters: Peter, Paul, Luke, Abigail, Hannah, Zapporah. When you live on a farm and there are lots of animals, you tend to emulate that Genesis-given role in naming them. This is what a Christian household looks like. So we named that llama James and John Sons of Thunder— and one would think it's fitting—the way it is but two names in one llama, a mirroring of the Trinity in a lesser form. A symbol for Christ's "fully God, yet fully man" personhood. But my brothers and I always joked it referred to his testicles: those sons of Thunder. Those sons who would bulge in the summer heat, who would shrivel on crisp mornings. Those sons who drove him to straddle the fence-line in pursuit of the females. And led to his castration. That day the vet cut them out, scalpeling the sack and loosening them from their hold, my brothers and I felt sadness in our hearts—like witnessing a funeral. Two little orbs emerged, cupped from the heat, white like a molded sphere of dried candle wax. I watched them disappear into the woods-line. (Did you know they bounce?) The llama's head limp from anesthesia, tongue flaccid in the barn floor dust. Now he's just called Thunder.

FROM Sixfold

DANIEL LASSELL

* * *

An Account of a Llama's Death

Zapporah died two days ago. She was a good llama. The way she watched over the newborn crias as they matured to adulthood. The way she guarded the herd at night against coyotes. She was so kind even to the youngest of my siblings. My father tied her body to the bush-hog and dragged her to a pit beneath the big tree at the end of our property, the family gravesite where all our animals rested. There, he cut the engine and tussled her through the snow into the hole. My brothers and I looked into the earth at her stiffened bulk, already losing wool. She was ripe with age, and had outlived many younger than her. She was full-blooded Chilean after all—one of the last imports before open trade stopped in '88. We had long hoped against this day. We shoveled dirt to blanket her from the winter. Clouds rolled on the horizon to drag a cold front in.

FROM SIXFOLD

LYN LIFSHIN

* * *

Thirty Miles West of Chicago

paint chips slowly.
It's so still you
can almost hear it
pull from a porch.

Cold grass claws
like fingers in a
wolf moon. A man
stands in corn bristles

listening, watching
as if something
could grow from
putting a dead child

in the ground.

FROM South Carolina Review

* * *

Nothing is haunted

in quite the way small Midwestern farms
are haunted. Girls, whip-thin in cotton nightclothes,
lie awake through summer's liquid heat and listen

to the rattling window screens, the drumming
warp of pie tins meant to drive blackbirds
from the strawberry beds. Lines of sweat

bead along their skin as the stalks bend
under the weight of whatever animal skirts
the edge of the field planted right up to the shed,

not a penny's worth of good dirt wasted by the men
who sleep the sleep of the damned or the nearly dead.
The handful of cattle corralled in the pen shuffle

and huff. They gnaw on rotten apples, eating
until they bloat and moan. The girls throw off
their bleached sheets and untangle their legs.

*

Their muscles urge them to bolt, yet they huddle and guard
themselves with the flick of the lamp's loosening switch, quivering
in one weak circle of light.

FROM *THE GIRLHOOD BOOK OF PRAIRIE MYTHS*
(JACAR PRESS)

KIM LOZANO

* * *

At the Titanic Museum

you can lower your hand into a tank of water
that's the same temperature as the water in the North Atlantic
on the night of April 14, 1912.

Placards fixed like headstones line the walls of the play room—
Step into the Captains Bridge and Steer the Ship
Sit in a Lifeboat
Try to Climb the Sloping Decks of Titanic

The third class cabin, the Grand Staircase,
the replica dinner plates and deck chairs
conjure up all that went down—
three-thousand bags of mail, thirteen unfinished honeymoons,
toddlers with tummies full of stewed apricots and currant buns
who watched the stern rise into the sky like the end
of a teeter-totter in that small spot of ocean
that's forever their own,

like this snowy hill in my town where my children are sledding
is forever ours. With coat cuffs secure at their wrists
they pull up their knees and glide down the slope where the earth
is breaking through under the sun.

I stick my ungloved hands in my pockets
and touch the souvenir boarding pass while my children
climb back up to me, their faces sparkling like glitter on water.

FROM *Valparaiso Poetry Review*

SANDRA MARCHETTI

* * *

Autumn Damask

Come.
Let me show you
the blown open roses
of nearly November.

Geese land in a card deck shuffle.
Their fingers sweep the ground
then plait down the body.

Lie fetal on the ground.
In the Midwest you will see
the world split—
a lidded eye drawn open as if
by marionette leads.

The willows are four crowns pointing down.

Comfort is when
you are tethered
to a place
you couldn't move
fast from anyway.

*

Roam the ground where you are
mapped, flat and free, beneath
this sky, this new sea.

FROM *STIRRING: A LITERARY COLLECTION*
(SUNDRESS PUBLICATIONS)

ADRIAN MATEJKA

* * *

Unfunky UFO, 1981

The first Space Shuttle launch got delayed until Sunday,
so we watched the shuttle's return in class instead—
PS113's paunchy black & white rolled in, its antennae
adjusted sideways & down for better reception so the set
looked like a teenager after his love letter got returned
to sender. The same day, Garrett jacked my new pencil
box. The same day, Cynthia peed her jeans instead of going
to the bathroom & letting Garrett jack her pencil box.
Both of us, too upset to answer questions about space
flight, so we got sent to the back of the class. Me, smelling
like the kind of shame that starts bar fights on Tuesday
afternoons. She smelled like pee & denim. The shuttle
made its slick way back to Earth, peeling clouds from
the monochromatic sky & we all—even the back of the bus
& astronomically-marginal—were winners. American,
because a few days before, a failed songwriter put a bullet
in the President in the name of Jodie Foster after she
returned his love letter unopened. The shuttle looked
like a bullet, only with wings & a cockpit, & when it landed,
the class broke into applause & the teacher snatched
a thinning American flag from the corner, waved it back
& forth in honor of the President & those astronauts.

FROM Gulf Coast

CARLO MATOS

* * *

*Honey**

You could tell they weren't from around here by the way they spread their honey, with a finger instead of a spoon—all thin, pilling at the rug of bread. It was like the day she finally admitted she had Hitler mannerisms: those arms, the contortions, the albedo—even the way the sweat flew off her cheeks—the fact that she always seemed to be yelling: her spit, an electron planning its next escape. Already there were so many things she couldn't do—just to be on the safe side. She would never grow a mustache, for example, but, of course, now she really wanted one. She would never ride bikes under a blood sun elbowing down the horizon: a siphonophore with its chain of red bellies trawling the deepest sea. Luckily, although she had not always felt this way, adventure was no longer something you had to go out and find on tippy toes on the bikes the color of last year's foams; it's something that grows on you—a wax tough on the teeth—a hive wall, a symbiote. There was so much dead telemetry while she waited for the off chance the waters would come and float the relics of riverboats and steamships to her front lawn.

FROM *CLEAVER MAGAZINE*

* This year, the use of foams has been strictly forbidden.

ZACHARIAH MCVICKER

* * *

The Apostate's Addendum

When we speak of the grotesque, we must also speak of love. In the
    predawn blooding before daybreak, the red vixen's scream

Sounds like the murder of a child. But we know, in springtime, it's a
    call of longing. In Calcutta, the beggars blind their children

So they'll have more to eat. It is rare when love is saintly. Even if
    Jesus wasn't the son of God, the crown of thorns still tore

The skin from his godly head. When the grape vine died
    in midsummer, blue wasps fed on the night-black nidi for weeks.

When you can't tell whether your lover cries out of pain or desire,
    you ache the more for the body. It would be a lie

To say we are not fulfilled by what we inflict. When God allows Job
    to suffer the trials, it is because he is ruthless. We were made

In that image. The man with the gun in his mouth knows this most
    of all—that we prosper in the depravity of these mercenary days,

Buying our lives at the price of our lives. Speak then of the picked
    clean beauty of our chitinous souls, our dry starch hearts of husk.

*

In Tibet, monks give their death-readied bodies to buzzards. But
   they call them Dakini, or sky dancers. Find here the varnished

Gleam of the macabre—you buff it over, it's gunmetal, it'll take you
   home. Be good, traveler. There are still many things to see.

FROM 32 POEMS

TREY MOODY

* * *

Same-Day Resolution

Since the time spring
has been here, I've
allowed myself two things:
clouds filled with weather
and skies filled

with clouds. As each
offers a separate perspective
my brain's consoled only
on both sides. The train
that passes through town

barely stops. But because
of it, money is money and time
time. Funny, the way
decision dictates so much—
I'm hungry, generally,

consistently, at a quarter
past three, though
my stomach's filled
so slow I often forget
when I've forgotten to eat.

FROM BOSTON REVIEW

MATTHEW MURRAY

* * *

Child Sobbing at the Library

Suddenly the quiet, that empty jug,
is being filled
with crying. A child is sobbing: not the wailing
of a slapped kid,
and not the tearful screeching of demands
and whining. No,
it is a child crying for something lost
or broken, something
that will never be replaced.
I listen, loving
the sound, as I love a lone violin
or muted trumpet
slowly filling the bowl of silence.
It is the crying
that I've lost, and will never have
again. I want
that child to cry and cry for everything
I've lost, every love
I've squandered, everything I should've
done. Cry for
my deaf father sitting hunched
in front of his loud TV,
for the house on Kenmore Street, for the tea
we drank, falling in love,
for the novels I'll never read, for the great

paintings hanging unseen
all night in empty museums, for the cities
of the world—all
their joyful streets, all their terrors—
for the dead and the way
time shoves us along, ignoring every
protest. Cry child,
and let it be the song, trapped beneath
this flat bone,
here where my ribs come together.

FROM ESCAPE INTO LIFE

RICHARD NEWMAN

* * *

Digging up the Elephant Ears

"If you can't love each other, just pretend,"
my mother begged my younger brother and me
who punched each other in back of our Impala.
I couldn't help but think of them today
when digging up the elephant ears—bright stalks
arcing six feet into the air each summer
and leaves the size of banquet platters that nod
languidly in breezes and condescend
to human heights only in August heat,
and yet they rise from ugly hearts, their gnarled
pink-tentacled bulbs that split to colonize
more earth and multiply in dirty broods.
They are the opposite of us, who must
force ourselves to dig beneath each others'
ugliness for hearts that hint of goodness
and love, and after first frost rarely bother.
But we must love each other, our betters say,
even the student who showed up to class
in a tight T-shirt that read *Fuck 'em all—*
let my ovaries sort it out. Especially her,
and the one who told the dean I showed up drunk,
which I have yet to do. My brother quit
drinking, I'm told—I haven't spoken to
my mother or my brother in seven years

since we no longer bother to pretend.
Each fall I am a brute and hack fine limbs,
pitching the hearts in garbage bins for winter.
Both front and back yards now are full of holes,
the stalks and ears wilting on compost piles.
The neighbor stumbles drunk down the alley.
Beneath his dirt and puke, I sometimes see
the good. Sometimes it's easier to pretend.
Squirrels salvage the last of this year's garden
while silence gathers in the eastern skies,
the last few ears bending to strains of air.

FROM *BOULEVARD*

ANDREW S. NICHOLSON

* * *

Utopian Rewrite

Through the gap in the bead-board,
you see the red memento in the adjacent room.
It promises far-off souvenir shops, landmarks in rows
silvered in snow globes—
another landscape you could hold in your hand.

Snow falls on an undersea Rome
as you peer how the architect could resketch
those Italian steps and the sun.

A new sky, a new city,
he could raise the next wall atop decayed leaves.
Cutting window in wall, he could remake, erase—
bedroom wall, bedroom window, he could baptize you
with the secret of rooms,

the domesticity that confides.
He could cove you, the secret between you.
He could hide you away in an attic cubby-hole.

For the gentlest ethnographers, life
is a bed and a window and a friend come to visit,
with you, still in bedclothes, entertaining, propped
up on an elbow. How nice
to notice yourself amid a half-conscious offer

*

for Earl Gray tea or a snack
for your uninvited other, to glimpse your
right hand's gesture toward the open cracker packet.

How nice, the phone call from England.
A woman rings, says she never leaves her bedroom,
she never leaves, caught in the warm breath falling from her mouth.
Her breath cools, pools in her bedspread's crevasses,
mountains and sea, spreading over her world:

the spired cities of her world, her twelve exiles
trekking from the foot of her bed to the yellow, dry floor,
her dry prayer, she prays, her god's matter-of-fact Hebrew—

He says, *Get out.*
This is your opening. This is your chance

to get through that gap to the grassland outside
the city limits, get out,
to the place beyond border beside the red obelisk,

the sandstone obelisk where I'll change every rule.

FROM ELEVEN ELEVEN

DEONTE OSAYANDE

* * *

Stand Up until the Guns Stop

We stand here ready to battle to the death
in the living room of my home. I'm armed
and you are loaded with only the claws
that a squirrel could have. I know it's you.
We first met when I was shoveling snow
a day ago. You were digging for your nuts.

The woman upstairs screaming in fear of you,
my mother, days before looked her best friend
in the eye as she told her she fears I will never marry.
Her friend wonders why, while my mother looks at me
in a way saying she has seen me love a lot of broken.
In that moment I felt as if I were a cracking field of ice.

I've always been an ice cube inside of an oven,
failing at keeping cool. My temper has died down
but winning over the approval of others has never been
a point of success. Once I flirted with a girl by mentioning
that cows have best friends and they become seriously stressed
when they don't see each other for long periods of time.
Not a great way to reveal insecurities while eating steak.

*

So why tell this to a random animal that has broken into my home?
Last night in my headphones I was listening to stand up comedians
while the neighbors turned our street into guerrilla warfare.
I laughed until the bullets stopped, a peaceful madness of sorts.

Here you are, a fellow survivor of their guns, but a trespasser no less.
The violence no longer startles us like the thirtieth time you've seen
the jerk of neck from an Alabama tree, and we're from there. You
are making my mother jump like the first time my mother witnessed
a weapon. One of us has to go, and I believe I was in this home first.

FROM Camroc Press Review

RACHAEL PECKHAM

* * *

Aunt Moreen's Confession

"She was a victim of incest. It was nearly on her death
bed that she confided this."
— in a letter from my grandmother

There, in back of the sugar house. That first time, I was caught by the
arm in a game of what else, hide-and-seek. Clothes-lined. I weighed
nothing but I was good at slipping out of any hold. I thought it was
just a round of that, but then fingers pinched my lips—shh, Mo.
Just like that. My feet flexing, gouging the dirt. Inside my head
I could hear a buzzing. Later, they accused me of crying no one
found me. Don't be so sore, they said, it's just a game. And I could
barely walk the path to the house and up the stairs and into bed.
Pretending to sleep through breakfast, just sticking my chores on
'em. Can't you see, Ma? She couldn't. She and Daddy had their own
trouble, working the orchard. Always wheat to thrash, more sap to
boil, oaks to cut, nothing gets done without some doing. And there
I was, chasing after brothers like a boy herself, making her mama
mumble words like you and watch. I hid my soiled things in the
bottom of the burn barrel. And even if they'd been found, they'd
never get a second look. Not then. Somebody was always lighting
clothes and bed sheets, making long kite tails of cottony smoke
after the influenza scare and school was closed, when I had to stay
home and keep up this game of hide-and-seek and hush-up-now.
But look, they said, how much she misses school, a born teacher.
Guess I could've gone some other way but I had no more fight in
me, nothing left of me in that orchard, to everybody's wonder. Poor

Moreen, picked clean behind the burn barrel she pushed over one morning, torching one whole acre in a drought no less. Oh, they knew. Shuffling me from different wards, springing for a special nurse and then a blood transfusion, oh yes—this I knew, mixing blood with blood. You can shock me silent and put yours inside, take it all out and give it back again because I'm Moreen, with all its meanings—wished-for child, bitterness of the sea.

FROM *ABZ: A New Magazine of Poetry*

JAN PETTIT

* * *

How to Save the World

You don't want to flush
because of the water. Therefore,
you cannot shit. Then, of course,
you cannot eat. Nothing can be made
that uses a thing or leaves a stain and all
must proceed backward from there. You can see
where this is going—woman, then girl, then child
pulling her hands from the rabbit muff, pedaling
the Schwinn in reverse, the dog rising up from
under the tire to unchase the car, grandfather
slipping out of a straitjacket, smiling again.
Old house sheds its new green paint, nails
flying from fragrant beams. Soon enough
logging trucks back down curly roads,
men with saws are propping up trees,
magnificent trees held up with
just their hands, and now,
the silent forest, full
of saplings, animals
wandering backward,
finger of God
retracting.

FROM *WATER~STONE REVIEW*

MIKE PUICAN

* * *

Englewood in Bloom

He is a giant with the voice of a girl; he
sings. Englewood stands at the window
above the Apostolic Lighthouse Church,
dawn striating the avenue and all of its
regular and irregular red townhomes.
As with the young girls who ride giggling
up and down Front Street all night when they
should be home in bed—so it is with him:
"Work hard all your young days and find
yourself with your soul out among the
grey doves all night on a phone wire."

He is tired of April's smallness,
the little leaves. He thinks: Are those
snowbells or do I make them snowbells?
Are dreams little flowers of desire, like
the wallpaper designs repeating or
sidewalks made to expand and contract
with changes in temperature? A stockbroker
dances in a shifting wind, someone's saxophone
describes the world. A breeze slips
under Englewood's shirt and gropes for his heart.
Curious dawn—it goes on forever. He sings.

FROM AFTER HOURS

MARY QUADE

* * *

Rickey Henderson Breaks the Record for Stolen Bases in a Season

Milwaukee, 1982

I was there. I know it's true,
but memory starts someplace, then steps away and
runs for it. Over the details falls doubt—
that tarp covering the field's blades.
                                        I'm ten,
my first real game. Arriving in the stands, fans
find numbered seats. And when we leave,
I get a pennant. But in between?
A zero-pocked chart.
                          I remember
the A's Rickey Henderson on base. The dance of leading off,
pitcher turning, back and forth. He throws to first, plays
his role, and we play ours—traitors, wanting to catch history;
we boo our own. I don't remember this.
            I don't remember
wanting anything except home runs, so the man
up at the giant beer barrel can ride his chute
into the giant mug, the suds—released balloons. But
the wrong team's at bat. Perhaps I want
a sausage wrapped in foil. Or maybe all the sausages
since then have placed that sausage in my mind.
I know I didn't want what I couldn't have

expected, this blurred anecdote to share now over
beer and talk of baseball.
                              And what does
Henderson remember? Not me, a speck of kid near first,
about to watch him speed away. He remembers
a game just days before on his home field,
second base beckoning. The crowd awaits his gift. But
when he dives, the umpire calls him out. He'll tell
that bitter story for years.
                              The pitcher
tires of looking back; he must propel
the inning somewhere—
                              and then
Henderson is stealing—a few strides, a plunge—
I like this, like skipping a grade—
and the game stops. A ceremony, a man gives him
the base, stolen, yet earned. I know this.
                              I know this
is what is done. The robbed diamond, the base
alien in his grip, irrelevant—like what follows. Or maybe
what follows matters most. Despite the spectacle,
my team wins.
                   And Henderson keeps stealing, stealing—
one moment in one place, and in the next, transported,
not like recollection, that stumbling, but instead,
impatient prophecy, a thing known with certainty
because it hasn't happened yet.

FROM Smartish Pace

LAYNE RANSOM

* * *

Wolves

That's my problem, I don't ever think!
Good thing you're constantly saving,
pulling me back into our collective HELLYEAH
heart before I hopscotch into traffic
or piss off Joyce Carol Oates again.
It's amazing how good cheap pizza
tastes when you're not alone.
Our talk is all giddy gobbledigook but
leaving Ohio, we had no words
and I was trying not to smile
so big I'd break, scattering
my shrapnel past the combination
Dairy Queen KFC Long John Silver's
into the grease-trap grave of the Midwest.
If I could slap a title on this moment
it'd be EVERYONE I LOVE IS HERE.
In your blue room we cuddle up
to each other's sadness, we fist bump
over God's epitaph, we owlshit
outburst because we're weirdos

and that's what we do, we stick together
and when we howl we howl because we want
somebody else to make a goddamn racket
with us at this balls-out impossible sky.

FROM FORKLIFT, OHIO

NANCY REDDY

*   *   *

Divine and Mechanical Bodies

The year my sister turned into a crow
          I ran the cinder track around the football field for hours.
I stayed on after practice ended, after coach packed up

his whistle and his stopwatch, after the other girls changed back
          into sweats and carpooled home. At my house

          my sister gathered all the shiny things. She plucked
the buttons from our parkas and strung them from the bedposts,
          lined the closet doors with tinfoil and propped
the silver-plated serving trays along the dressers

so that everywhere she looked
she'd see her own eyes looking back. She wouldn't speak.

          When our mother called us down to dinner
she answered with a raucous preening call, she piled mall kiosk
          pendants around her feathered neck. She wouldn't eat

the meals our mother cooked and instead slurped juice from cans,
          clawed the soft and flaky centers from the caramels

in the cut-glass candy dish our mother kept for guests. She grew
bird-boned and slender, a brittle core inside each inky feather.

*

That year, though no one had died, not really,

my mother filled the basement freezer with casseroles,
        each aluminum dish an archaeological dig of hash browns,
beef tips browned in butter, cream of something soup. In bio lab

we pinned and bisected earthworms, diagrammed their tiny hearts
                on worksheets. Somewhere a teacher called out
        kingdom, phylum, family.

We smeared the cultured cells from petri dishes onto slides
and marveled at their manufactured one-cell lives. I ran the track
        each afternoon, my mix tape turned up loud. The sun set

earlier and earlier each day behind the goal posts. At home
my mother diced and browned the onions. My sister

        made herself a feather bed. The first snow
fell around us as we slept, flakes soft as down,
clotting the trees whose leaves had not yet
        turned and fallen, turning the lawn
bright as a spotlight.

FROM SMARTISH PACE

RITA MAE REESE

* * *

The Margin Is for the Holy Ghost

*Betty Hester's admonition to Flannery O'Connor, warning
her not to write in the borrowed copy of* The Notebooks of
Simone Weil. *Beginning lines are borrowed from* The
Notebooks.

1. Milledgeville

is the nothingness from which she flees
& the nothingness toward which she goes.
Is the frozen world of Parmenides
where she was raised & where she was returned,

where existence is uniform & unchanging,
where just down the road is the state asylum
where bad children are sent, where she
could still be sent if she's not careful,

where half of her was sent—her inner Hulga,
bloody fist knocking on sleeping doors.
To avoid the bloody fist she stays at her desk,
writing letters to friends who left home

& stayed gone, who live in the luxury of exile,
rooted to the absence of a definite place.

2. Manley Pointer's Sonnet

To be rooted in the absence of a definite place,
to be not from any place, just from near someplace,
is to carry always with you this portable altar
to the brokenness everyone tries to hide.

To know this world is held together only
with tape & glue & clumsy stitches,
to be driven from door to door selling snake's ink
is to be the loneliest boy in the lonely world,

the last emperor of clarity.
The altar grows heavier at each house—
all those glass eyes & wooden legs.
No one is ever glad to see you, but when you go

you leave them knowing everything
Pavlov's dogs & other martyrs know.

3. A Temple of the Holy Ghost

Pavlov's dogs & other martyrs know
that consciousness is a mirror
the body created to look at itself,
that each body is only a body

like all other bodies, mortal in every cell,
asking who is the finest? Know some spells
are never broken. The body a mirror too,
and between the mirrors a dollhouse

miniature of infinities. Know this world
is a wind of reflections tacking between
unlandable shores. Ask us who
isn't haunted by a reflection in search of

a mirror, unbound and determined now
to teach us to give in the spirit of one who begs?

4. J-O-B

To learn to give in the spirit of one who begs
means first you have to learn how to beg.
I think of my drunk friend telling
a homeless guy in DC: get a J-O-B.

A few years later, drunk again, hits a tree.
He told me once that his father would
come home drunk, come into his room
with a gun, threaten to blow his brains out.

He never said if he'd pretend to be asleep, cry,
plead, pray or how he'd get up the next day,
go to school, return to that room, lie down & wait.
If he knew why any man would want

to see his own son begging for his life.
The stories about miracles confuse everything.

5. There's Wood Enough Within

The stories about miracles confuse everything:
You awake to the wolf of Gubbio licking your hand,

St. Francis bringing you breakfast in bed.
Your room is the lion's den & you are Daniel.
Your room is a whale & you are Jonah,
Pinnochio, Ahab. The windows disappear,
the walls lean in. The walls of Jericho may fall
but not these walls. These walls are trees
& you are where someone loves you best
of all, your room is the woods & you
are only a girl, but a whole girl, a girl
without pain, standing still at the edge.

Then comes a knock like a flame catching the trees, & you,
poor wooden girl caught, as pain opens the door.

6. A Bird Sanctuary

The pain that opens the door
sometimes opens windows too.
You lie on the floor as if
you're floating on a sea of board.

You watch the birds fly in. All you want
is for them to pick you clean.
Instead they make nests, lay eggs,
raise their feathered young. You pluck

out your hair, one by one. Blind fingers find
each loose thread and pull. You pick
yourself clean. The floor is cool and smooth,
the air is filled with flight patterns

*

and something like happiness in between:
a usage for every kind of error.

7. Everything that Rises

There is   a usage for every kind of error
& you're still asking what yours will be.
It is one of your weaknesses that you believe
someone or something can spin you into gold.

The black dog at the foot of the bed stirs,
digs a hole to bury you. Nothing to do
but lie still, taste dirt. Nothing will save you
from tragedy except comedy, which is worse.

Let the ground find a use for your body
which was my home, which was never my home.
Let your words sink beneath your tongue
which was my root.

Close your eyes & let the nothingness
from which you flee be the nothingness

FROM JUBILAT

MARGARET ROSS

* * *

In Parts Unknown

Then any sense of where we were
gone. Then gulls like paper
angels sat on their masts
for a while. Foam on the water
laced maps whose every route

unraveled. "Then" unraveled. Routes
retraced as frothing monsters
sketched in the margin by faith
that fear took forms men had
devised for it. Where

does the time go? Steered by
balancing his thoughts
against imagined ground, in this
way holding it steady
open-winged as beech

moths pinned to carry home
for evidence. Faith sailed
on white silk panels of a dress
she wore the day he left
whispering Imagine that

*

you are already coming home
to me. If not angels, then specimens
of lichen pressed inside
my book imprinting wingspan
silhouettes against the words "appeared

to me in an excess of mind, in a
dream, before the doors" in fainter colors
than nightjars outside this window
carried by wind towards trees
tall as ships. Not only hours

but miles can be rigged
like this to vanish under cell phone
towers extinguishing the ground
you would be forced to cross
to speak with me

face to face. There isn't time
enough. Make the proof yourself.
Each grain is the head
of a nail pinning nothing to
nothing, by which I mean holding

the time up. That ticking is
just static. The clock is waiting
to ring. The shore they reached
finally was sifted grain
from their dreaming

*

eyes. Can you hear? I'm saying
I believe every step: five girls
in white leotards climb into
a tall-case clock. The door
is shut. The clock is spun around. Then

a small boy pushes
the pale face out. And the glass
case where the gold spines swing
he pushes it out. Sets these
parts on the stage. Then seeing

the spare wood frame
is hollow, slender as a wrist
on every side, a door, or, "Here begins
the Book of Visions. Imagine that
you are on the road to Paradise."

FROM FENCE

MARGARET ROSS

* * *

Burrow

If grass explains what is invisible
beneath it, each blade in shorthand

spells a corresponding channel
cut, continuing below

the dirt's horizon, and is no grave.
The muscles underground

exceed their animals, extruding
tunneled wakes. As phosphenes flare

beyond the retina's range
yet wear its colors. As pygmy mice

that nightly set a pebble wall
to seal their burrow's entrance.

The field's grass phalanx
quivers as it stays

itself against all shadow, feather,
breeze, fur, shifting

*

surface light, expanse, each flimsy
arrow leveled at indifference.

FROM BOSTON REVIEW

MARY KAY RUMMEL

* * *

Palimpsest

If by truth you mean hands
shaping the vertebrae of stars

If by hands you mean oak branches
scratching the moon's face

If by branches you mean that sickle moon
lying on its side as if asking

If by moon you mean pillow, expectant
as we, fingers laced, walk dim streets

If by pillow you mean feather words
the breath of fasting lovers

If by words you mean answers
where the moon tilts on its side
like a burning blade

If by answer you mean bruised trees,
clouds, lights of a far-off city, or the way
your finger slides into my closed fist

*

trembling the lifeline, the way
your palms resurrect my breasts.

FROM *ASKEW*

JUSTIN RUNGE

* * *

History

Here is what I've collected: He set fire to the front lawn. She learned and then forgot the guitar. Like all daughters, she was a vegetarian. He was sent to school on the mountain. She would run through the mountain. Their siblings stood in the way. The mountain was beautiful but merciless, with trees like chaperones. He took to botany. She slept in the haunted room. After the growth spurt, he was a natural athlete. She worked at a fast food restaurant. Both left without diplomas. He sat in a bunker, catching moths. She would walk to a payphone in the center of town. They would solve crossword puzzles days late. He left on a motorcycle, as in his favorite songs. They married on her birthday. Her hair was never longer. She escaped a home imploding. He had a television and a frying pan. They made mistakes—pepper oil, poison ivy. They had one child, then me.

FROM RATTLE

NATALIE SHAPERO

* * *

Invocation: The Third and Fourth Generation of Them That Hate Me

All you need for a piano is a tree
and an elephant. I sit up sick and humming
K381, which means I am like Mozart,
having heard the music once and now
it is in me. Mozart had his harpsichord,
I have my ugly mouth. I whistle
at my plants to make them smarter.
I learn from them that Sistine
is the adjective of Sixtus. I learn from them
that Mozart was atrociously behaved,
and the pope was always angry, and the devil
was always angry, and you can't make
something flower using force, and the sins
you undertake alone will only turn you coarse.

How difficult to be a rare animal,
the pressure to stay alive. Even colors find
themselves in danger, blue eyes
that should have died out by now,
spare in their occurrence to begin with
but passed on against the odds. This can only
mean it's common to seek a blue-eyed lover.
Yes, I too have done it. I am, as the Icarus

unveiled at the wax museum, highly
lifelike. I highly like life, though in a faraway
and pent-up manner, in the way of the assassin
pining for the actress. His common
letters I have sat up reading, mouthing out
the worst of them as though
in peaceable worship of a genius teen oh DON'T
YOU MAYBE LIKE ME A LITTLE BIT? YOU MUST
ADMIT IT I AM DIFFERENT.

FROM FENCE

NATALIE SHAPERO

* * *

I Don't Sleep in White

Religion being defined as the expectation
of future punishments, my people
sat in prayer. They sat on thatch and slashed their hair
in marriage, traveled under Gothic names
with papers sewn in the lining of their coats. I came
late, talked late, misunderstood their jokes,
those punch lines that entailed a working
comprehension of old world exchange
rates. I never prayed to God, but begged the clouds
to meet my needs: not rain, form scenes
from favored books. I was put into acting as a child,
carried by other children over the lake
of fire we were instructed to imagine. Student of ash,
I grew up fleck-complected, short of breath. I set
out seeds for small birds, watched them eat
their weight, watched others do the same. Though
I've been told white suits me, I don't sleep in white.
My bad eyes in the morning can't discern a shirt
from bedding. I am through with needing
to have such fabric handed to me, turned out
like the turned out feet of birds. Cloud, have mercy
on these small destructions. Send me to a war, I'll leave
the war. Sharpen my want of dying, I won't die.
Cloud, believe I once believed in justice.

I thought it was a bird that I could wait for: coffee
thermos, special lenses, drabbest coat at dawn.
I thought if I was quiet, I would see it. Cloud, forgive
the error. Cloud, forget the branches I have broken
in my terror. Cloud, have only patience with the lover
presenting his nakedness like the unpainted
puzzle they gave in grade school
to test if we were smart. Cloud, I was always
smart. Where has it gotten me? Haven't I
lived correctly? Haven't I fed whatever asked to be,
felt only fear of creatures whose refusal to fear me
evinced a rabidness? Why can't I be
like my grandfather, wear a heavy hat,
play Baltic anthems on the violin and just expect
that those with whom I share my life will know
how many kopeks in a ruble? My error was trusting
in acting, and sleeping in white, and building homes
for shadow birds, which means I have built homes for
many hands. There are so many kopeks in a ruble.
Cloud, there are more than you can ever know.

FROM THE PROGRESSIVE

PHILIPPE SHILS

* * *

the brain surgeon

he said parts
of her brain
would be
like gossamer

and that would
help guide him
to the parts
that are not
like gossamer.

he seemed
competent and
the word gossamer
seemed impractical
and poetic

and I trusted
him then.

FROM *Sixth Finch*

MAGGIE SMITH

* * *

This Town

You might tell yourself you want to leave. Hell,
you might want to leave. This town, this stinking town,

the woods and cornfields that lured you from home
late at night while your parents slept, bulldozed

for strip malls and surface parking. Once you could lie
in the tall grass with the boy you loved, the deer

just feet away, and never be found. You haven't been
kissed like that in years, pressed to the earth in a place

you called nowhere because there was nothing
to fence in. You might have dreamt it except for

the details: the taste of drugstore wine, the speckled
fawn staring, not even flicking an ear. Acorns

pinged a barn roof and rolled in the gutters
like arcade pinballs. Bats darted at the treeline,

half-drunk, hungry for your hair. Face it, your life
is not what it was. The boy you loved is a dozen

*

years behind you, whatever that translates to in miles.
He's married to someone else and has a daughter,

and so do you. His parents don't live in the house
you crept to, the house in the sticks. Teenagers now

can't have what you had in this town—nowheres
all along Old 3-C highway, hawks appearing wherever

you went like a talisman, the crickets in stereo,
tricking you into believing they had you surrounded.

But the creek still runs cold behind the house
where your parents raised you, where they live,

and the deer still find their way to the backyard
somehow, deep in the suburbs. They materialize

behind the house and just as quickly, they're gone.

FROM DIODE

MAGGIE SMITH

* * *

Marked

They are alone, the woman and the girl child.
The man has gone over the mountain

to work for a year, maybe longer, and the sunlight
here is a little bitter, the color of turmeric,

the same gold as the leaves floating down.
The girl has an eye like a spyglass for birds.

She must be marked, the woman thinks.
Wherever she walks, the shadow of a hawk

falls on her, the way a light trains on something.
In this thick forest, light can't touch

every leaf, but the woman watches
wind touch all of them. If they weren't paper-

thin, this rustling would be a hammering
like hooves on hard ground. The man will return,

but what a strange homecoming to the world
belonging to the woman and child. They cut

*

its intricate shapes from nothing, like silhouettes
from paper. They have a rhythm. Mornings

to the creek on horseback, ocher leaves falling
through ocher air nearly indistinguishable.

Evenings, at the fire, telling stories the man
won't know. Maybe there is something about

his hands, rough as bark, the girl will remember.
But if she's grown wild in this wilderness,

who could blame her. Once small enough
to fit inside the hawk's fallen shadow,

now she can almost outrun it, only the dark
blade of a wingtip scissoring across her face.

FROM THE SOUTHERN REVIEW

ROBERT STEWART

* * *

Aves

My wife has been cut open
	five times—not the times
of love, *Welcome, welcome;*
	my boat wallows in the sea—
the times of laparoscopy
	and three sections casting
scars like ladder rungs
	against a tree, or the rings
of that tree documenting
	times of rainfall or lack
of rainfall, her story tattooed
	and not easily translated
across her abs, the spans
	of pale birds some countries
call *aves*, lifting themselves
	like veils until *look*, this
cut, now, to remove the womb,
	an ooze of blood on gauze
where the staples gave.

	So daily I flush with saline
the salmon-colored aspect
	we expect our divinity
to have of itself, an *ave,*

fruitful and full of grace
the depth of the wound,
        healing from inside out
and measured by a Q-tip
        the width of my thumb.
I pack wound-filler tape
        as an apprentice plumber,
packing oakum into bells
        of caste-iron pipe. Flesh
spreads and closes itself,
        no pour of molten lead
to hold back all-too-much
        evidence of time before us—
muscles and corpuscles,
        pulpy as the flesh of plums,
lying sweetly in the grass.

If I mention the home-care
        nurse, Faith, who taught me
to wash and pack a wound,
        someone will say, Being
makes us strong; the galvanized,
        turned-over bucket my wife
needs to step into the truck raises
        her esteem; and someone
will say *stigmata*, a holiness
        visible or aching to reveal
this place & time in Paul's letter,
        I bear on my body the marks;
my teachers, Dominican nuns
        at Little Flower School, covered
all but their hands and faces,

but wore beads at their sides
and fingered as they walked
        five *aves* for each *pater noster.*

The proof made flesh lies
        in clouds beginning to rotate
buildings south of here; or
        a little girl I can't forget
still running on a road in war
        directly at us, her arms
forming a cross on fire.
        Let us pray. I have what lies
before me morning and night,
        a woman cut open like a pink
line on a horizon, from which,
        fallen, glowing, we are told,
blessed is the fruit—this soiled
        packing cloth, a sign of blood
for the health of the wound,
        the time given us to turn
inward, healing body first.

FROM Marimar

JESSICA THOMPSON

* * *

History

The day Neil Armstrong walked on the moon,
we dug for treasure in a dumpsite on the farm

where she moved after they left the coalfields
of Eastern Kentucky. I married her son,

the one who came late in life, the one who
waited until after the bleeding had stopped.

We found shards of pottery, pieces
of china caked in black dirt, but nothing

that had not been broken. Divorced and
dead for thirty years, her boy still haunts me.

He speaks to a girl I no longer recognize.
She pleads with me to keep digging

for that which was lost, to find the thing
not meant to be thrown away,

*

that which stirs

beneath the blunt blade of a shovel.

{ 201 }

FROM *KUDZU*

JEFF TIGCHELAAR

* * *

A Report on Love and Wrestling

Love and Wrestling first came to Massachusetts
In the Year of Our Lord 1620. The quarters were tight
On the Mayflower. Love was about
Nine years old; Wrestling,
A little bit younger.

Love and Wrestling were brothers.
Their father, William Brewster, was the leader of the
Separatists.
When Love and Wrestling were in their youth,
America hadn't even been born. The country was yet just
A spangle in its mother's weary eye.

Love and Wrestling were known to frolic
In the fields of Plymouth Plantation.
They managed to survive
Those terrible winters, and even the Indians
Proved friendly. By this time Fear had already arrived.
And also Jonathan.
Patience was longer in coming.

*

It came to pass that Love grew up.
He married, and fathered four children.
We know much less about Wrestling.

FROM PLEIADES

JEFF TIGCHELAAR

* * *

Why Won't You Be Real with Us?

they asked. And what he didn't say
was: I've got two tons of smog in my heart

and every now and then I shave
my face into a half moustache
and stay inside the house a few days

FROM THRUSH POETRY JOURNAL

LEE UPTON

* * *

Love's Ode

There once was a man who loved me
with a cat's love,
which is to say I could not depend on it,
although I could depend on his punctuality.

A cat's appetite is a clock.
There once was a clock
who loved me like a man.
Not like any man

but like one particular man.
A clock has time on its hands
and you can tell time's up by its face.
There once was a face

that loved me like a suitcase,
a suitcase on the conveyor belt
forgotten for two weeks at the airport.
There once was a man

who loved me like an airport.
I had to take off my clothes
just to get past security.
There once was security

*

in loving no one at all.
No one at all was enough for me.
Then I bought a cat.
A man appeared who loved me

as if he loved me.
Love was a cat in a clock in a suitcase
passing through airport security.
I risked so much, it's beyond me.

FROM RIVER STYX

WENDY VARDAMAN

* * *

American Love Poem after Oz

1.   The way a person leaving becomes loved.

2.   The way Aunt Em did not run after Dorothy before shutting
     the cellar door between them.

3.   The way an older woman worries the strap of her little black
     purse and folds her arms across it on her wide, white lap.

4.   The way a house makes a house-shaped hole in the heart-
     shaped heart.

5.   The way someone who is rusty still draws a bow straight
     across each string.

6.   The way Aunt Em was once that girl she won't run after.

7.   The way a face sparkles with moonlight bouncing off its
     metal.

8.   The way you won't you will you won't you will begin again.

9.   The way Aunt Em thinks folks will laugh at her socks.

10. The way Dorothy becomes a woman who worries over an
     uninsured package.

11. The way a soldier, even victorious, will have to get home.

12. The way magic matters, the way wizards lie.

13. The way Dorothy requires Aunt Em requires Dorothy
     requires—

14. The way awe requires you until you require awe.

15. The way a house crushes.

FROM *MUSEUM OF AMERICANA*

LISA VIHOS

* * *

Pumpkin Seeds

We are all together again
on Halloween eve
just like always, me
up to my elbows in pumpkin guts,
you and your dad
at the table, seated
before spread-out newsprint.

Divorce is irrelevant
when there are pumpkins to carve.
I attack another
with the largest kitchen knife I own,
in imitation of a bad horror movie.
How pale and vulnerable
my wrists are. I am crazy

for the seeds. The seeds
are the only reason I carve pumpkins
anymore. Well, and to see what you—
at your age—might make. Interwoven
throughout one stringy womb,
I find sprouted seeds, a pumpkin
pregnant with fledgling

*

jack-o-lanterns of the future;
lit and grimacing faces that will
never be, maniacal grins for porches
we can only imagine. Then, I tell you
a story: the autumn you were in utero,
my first trimester, I craved pumpkin seeds,
and your dad brought them to me by the bowlful.

In fact, you are probably 95 percent pumpkin seed
I say and you say, *I don't really like them!*
We laugh, we three, around our table. Then,
we light candles, place them inside the hollows
we have made. Just like us, they flicker and wink
at decay. Cleaned and carved by loving hands,
the very faces of creation.

FROM VERSE WISCONSIN ONLINE

ANGELA VORAS-HILLS

* * *

Itch

The nag tail-whipped flies from her back,
boys jumped from boats into rushes
to avoid being bitten. Even cranes left eggs

to hatch untended off marshy, wooded trails. So,
when our swatter's waffle-holes jellied yellow and red,

it was impossible to know whose blood it was.

The man lying on shore watched the boys
splash, disappear, while filling his mouth with flies,
then spiders, sparrows, like the old woman

who'd swallow anything living
to get rid of the tickle inside her.

But this has nothing to do with gain

or the soul's weight: it's about heat—
The train carries a woman in a winter coat,
carrying dirty bags full of dirty bags and empty bottles.

This is silently about the flies pouring from a slit
along the seam of her coat as she stands,

*

whispering: this is my blood, this

is my cup, and the secret way
I inch a pen down the back of my throat
to scratch out the ink of their crawling.

FROM Cimarron Review

DONNA VORREYER

* * *

Bringing in the Sheaves

You chase me through a cornfield
and we surface in a clearing, all
that we know and do not know
shimmering between us, invisible
door with no knob or hinges, no
way to open or close. You can only
stare at the horizon. Hidden in

the stalks, crickets sing. I rub
my thighs together in bold
commiseration. A thousand ears
listen for answers that do not come.
I do not know what you want. I do
not know what I want. I begin to
tear at tassels, braid the pulled silk

into a gown the color of your hair.
You shrug, turn and motion for me
to follow you back. I cannot find
my way through that door, so I run
in the other direction, gown streaming
above my head like a banner. All that

is left is my rustle, the black confetti
of crickets littering the sky in my wake.

FROM *APPLE VALLEY REVIEW*

JOE WEINTRAUB

* * *

The Catch

"No man is an island, entire of itself; every man
is a piece of the continent, a part of the main."
— John Donne, Devotion XVII

Of course, it wasn't at all like Willie Mays
    in flight, his back to home, or Reiser's bouts with the wall;
yet still, with body outstretched, my glove upraised,
the ball in slow descent, the ground, a shock, and a roll,
and back on my feet, the final out in hand,
one Holy Jesus of a catch that Don would recall
forever, he later said, until the sands
of time ran down; and as my winning team
swarmed over me, he abandoned the field,
head bowed, to retrieve his bat and to yield
the glory—that with swing and contact seemed
to be his at first—to me. He drowned
the following year. A slip and fall overboard,
his head cracking on the rail, corpse found
a day or so later, floating just off the shore;
and now I'm left alone with the memory, mine
alone, without a witness (the others, in time,
have all forgotten), a memory that fades

into a dream of that wondrous catch I made
so many years ago, with the game on the line.

FROM *AFTER HOURS*

MARK WILLIAMS

* * *

Identity Theft

1.

It's June and I can't WAIT for our new crepe myrtle to bloom!
I've forgotten the variety of our new crepe myrtle.
I could ask my wife.
But by not knowing the name of our new crepe myrtle,
I don't know the color its blooms—
which only ADDS to my excitement! Not only that,
my wife said I can have another gazing ball—
to complement our new crepe myrtle!
Plus, we have a CONSPICUOUS gap in our hydrangeas!

I once climbed the Grand Teton.

2.

One day a man is walking his dog through a leafy park
when he sees a girl with a snake around her neck.
The snake's name is Noah. Noah the boa.
Only the man doesn't know Noah the boa's name
when he finds himself forming some *pret-ty* definite opinions
about the girl with purple-black hair and skin
the color of no color whatsoever, excluding
the surfeit of tattoos, the gold and silver rings

and pins on her pale canvas.
But the thing about this man, opinions or not,
he can't help but talk. In addition to Noah's name,
he learns Noah's body temperature approximates surrounding air,
so, no, Noah doesn't cool the girl on hot days. Surprisingly,
the girl works at the psychiatric hospital through the leafy trees
where she takes Noah on her days off to cheer the cheerless.
Also, Noah the 23-year-old, affectionate boa
came from a Rosy Boa rescue,
which makes him feel not so rosy—the man—
since, now, *all* of his *pret-ty* definite opinions
are *pret-ty* definitely wrong.
Soon the man is expressing his displeasure
with the Frisbee golf course that violates the leafy trees,
when, despite their disparity in age, pets, skin tone, etc.,
the girl suddenly says,
                    I feel ya,
to which the clueless man replies,
                              Uh, no thanks.

Some days the man feels like a nameless crepe myrtle
that has forgotten the color of its blooms.

3.

My Grandma Mabel had an aunt named Myrtle.

4.

It's 1969 and I'm at a Nashville honky-tonk with my friend Norman.
Norman and I are eighteen. In four years,
Norman will become a Nashville cop. One night
he'll pull me over in my Pinto and ask to see my license.

Hey, Norman. It's me, I'll say. But tonight
Norman already has a license *and* a social security card
for one William B. Robinson, age 21 plus.
Wh Y, you bo-oys have the say-m nay-m!
our waitress says after careful study.
Norman will matriculate to Vanderbilt Law.
He'll become a prominent defense attorney.
We're fraternal twins, Norman tells the waitress.
I'm William Butler Robinson,
and he's my brother, William Blake.

Ye-ah, and I'm Tammy WY-nette, the waitress says.

5.

My mother's maiden name was Angel. Martha Jeanne Angel.
I was an angel before I met your dad, my mother liked to say.

6.

One day the man is stopped at a stoplight near the leafy park
(where he seems to spend a lot of time),
when he notices a girl in a giant red pick-up
with a young man's hands around her neck.
The young man's name is Tim, Tim as in
Get your hands OFF me, Tim!   Tim. Once again,
the man finds himself forming some *pret-ty* definite opinions
when the girl jumps from the giant red pick-up
and starts running down the leafy street
and Tim jumps from the giant red pick-up
and starts running down the leafy street, too.
Naturally, the man can't help but talk.

{ 219 }

*

But this time his talking must wait until the light turns green
and he drives around the block listening to someone say,
You just can't drive away, you miserable coward!—
bearing in mind there is no one with him in his car.
Later that night he tells his wife what he *did* say
after he rounds the block and follows the re-occupied, giant red
    pick-up
to *Emergency Parking* at a nearby hospital—
which doesn't make the miserable coward feel any less miserable
or cowardly.

7.

Man: (*knocking on passenger-side window of a giant red pick-up*)

    Are you OK?

Girl: (*rolling down window*)

    Yes. Thanks.

Tim: (*jumping from driver's side of the giant red pick-up,
    siren blaring in the background*)

    Who the hell are you!

Man: I just want to make sure she's OK.

Tim: (*balling his fists*)

    You might want to leave us alone, m______ f______!

*

Man: I just want to make sure you're both OK.

LATER THAT DAY

Wife: (*watering blue hydrangeas*)

He never would have hit someone your age.

8.

Some days it seems impossible to the man
that he is 23 in Rosy Boa years.
That no one will ever hit him hard right between the eyes.

9.

If you don't know me by now,
You will never never never know me, ooh, ooh-ooh-ooh-ooh.

10.

If the last 23 years were an illusion,
Simply Red would be singing If You Don't Know Me By Now,
Noah the boa would be about seven inches long,
and I would be showing this poem to my gentle friend and mentor,
the exquisite formalist poet, Mike Carson,
who would undoubtedly return it to me with the word *DECORUM!*
written in the right-hand margin of Part 7—
since I would have undoubtedly filled the blanks in.
Never mind Tim the angry, giant red pick-up driver,
or rather angry Tim, the giant—Oh, you know what I mean—

filled the blanks in, too. Never mind Tim is not alive
and pick-ups aren't so giant.

If the last 23 years were *not* an illusion,
Tim *would* be alive, pick-ups *would* be giant
and I'd be asking when you last heard the word *decorum*?
If you find it kind of nice to hear the word *decorum*
and wish there were precious more of it going around,
chances are you had a grandmother and great-great aunt
with names like Mabel and Myrtle. Chances are
you sometimes forget the color of your blooms.

11.

Some days I can't believe I've become someone
who longs for the days when more decorum was going around,
someone who uses long as a verb and precious at all.

Some days I can't believe my knees have wrinkles.
That I count lawn mowing as exercise.
That my mower's self-propelled.

Some days I can't believe I still say, *honky-tonk.*
That I plant *blue* hydrangeas.
That both my mother and my dad are angels now.

12.

It's 2012 and I'm at a funeral home telling my friend Norman
that I'm sorry about his mother, Pearl.
It's been many years since I've seen Norman. Of course
we'll talk about the time he pulled me over in my Pinto.

The time we hiked The Appalachian Trail.
I once hiked The Appalachian Trail.)
This is my friend, William Blake Robinson,
smiling Norman tells his granddaughter.
It's nice to meet you Mr. Robinson,
smiling Norman's smiling granddaughter says.

13.

One day in 1704, a man appeared in England.
He claimed to be Prince George Psalmanazar, reformed cannibal
from the island of Formosa—where men ate adulterous wives,
18,000 baby boys were sacrificed each year to an elephant god,
and everyone wore snakes around their necks TO KEEP THEM COOL!
Little wonder *A Historical and Geographical Description of Formosa,*
An Island Subject to the Emperor of Japan was a bestseller.
When a Jesuit missionary from Formosa asked about his fair skin,
Psalmanazar claimed he'd always lived beneath the ground.
Sunlight would shine directly down an equatorial chimney,
the astronomer Edmond Halley reasoned.
Formosan chimneys are almost always built at crooked angles
and containing bends, Psalmanazar rebutted.
Ye-ah, and I'm Tammy WY-nette,
Sir Edmond might as well have said.

14.

Well, I hit him hard right between the eyes
And he went down, but to my surprise,
He come up with a knife and cut off a piece a my ear.

15.

If the last 43 years were an illusion,
Johnny Cash would be singing *A Boy Named Sue*
on the jukebox in the Nashville honky-tonk
where I'm drinking beer with my friend Norman,
thanks to the likes of Tammy Wynette.
In four years I'll get a job in a psychiatric hospital
and acquire a life-long soft spot for those who cheer the cheerless.
After that, I'll climb the Grand Teton, hike The Appalachian Trail
and develop an interest in ornamental shrubbery—
which will lead to a delight in gazing balls.
One day I'll gaze into my favorite,
the deep blue ball with light green swirls.
I'll find it hard to believe I've become someone
who gazes into a deep blue ball with light green swirls,
especially with the likes of William Blake
drinking Old Milwaukee Beer in a Nashville honky-tonk,
signaling to Tammy Wynette but gazing out at me
and saying,
   Who the hell are you?

FROM Rattle

* * *

XXVIII. Learning Aid

7 february

dear simon warren, digging through a bin at the recycle center i found a book, the inside cover inscribed—dalton elmore—in childish script, copyright 1981. dalton, then, is doubtless grown, and if following the expected order of things, married with daltons of his own. on the other hand dalton elmore may be with us no more. he may be on the other side. he may be very much beyond us now.

imagine, in this case, the case of the absent boy, a room perfectly preserved, the boyhood things neatly placed. imagine the book i found in the bin among these things. it s about bugs. i carried it home for my own shelves. but imagine the case of an absent boy, the boyhood room cleaned out, dalton s parents perhaps having turned over a new leaf. or, perhaps being absent themselves, having simply gone on to whatever the next thing is.

how good of them, in either case, to preserve dalton s book until the very last moment so i can read that insects have no lungs, but holes and tubes, that they have no nose but hairlike things with which they smell, that they taste with antennae or the undersides of their feet. in the back of the book is an ad for a learning aid that challenges a youngster to go beyond and another for bookshelves

of walnut or oak, the real meaning of stability. i remember, in
another life, thinking some things went on forever.

there s a drawing of a little boy, hands in the dark air, points of light
swirling like van gogh s stars. let me tell you now what i ve learned.
some kinds of fireflies don t eat, they mate and then they die, but
o my god, the larva—the horror—the larva creeps with its belly
along the earth and poisons prey with its mouthparts. let me tell
you, the hornets, by summer s end when the nest is dry, the males
and princesses fly away and they do not return. i ve not heard from
you in some time.

FROM Apple Valley Review

CONTRIBUTOR BIOGRAPHIES

LINDSEY ALEXANDER's work has also appeared or is forthcoming in *Colorado Review*, *Green Mountains Review*, and *DIAGRAM*. She recently moved to east Tennessee from Indiana, where she received an MFA in poetry from Purdue and her bachelor's degree from IU.

NIN ANDREWS is the author of six chapbooks and five full-length collections of poetry. Her next book, *Why God Is a Woman*, is forthcoming from BOA.

KATE ANGUS's work has appeared in *Indiana Review*, *Subtropics*, *Court Green*, *The Awl*, *The Hairpin*, *The Rumpus*, *Verse Daily*, and *Best New Poets 2010* and *2014*. She is the recipient of A Room of Her Own Foundation's "Orlando" Prize, *The Southeast Review*'s Narrative Nonfiction prize, and an artists residency on the Wildfjords trail in Iceland. A former Writer in Residence at Interlochen Arts Academy, she currently lives in New York where she is a founding editor of Augury Books and serves as the Creative Writing Advisory Board Member for The Mayapple Center for Arts and Humanities.

ROBERT ARCHAMBEAU's books include *The Poet Resigns* (Akron), *Laureates and Heretics* (Notre Dame), *Home and Variations* (Salt), *Word Play Place* (Ohio), and others. He has received awards from the Academy of American Poets, the Illinois Arts Council, and the Swedish Academy. He is professor of English at Lake Forest College and blogs at Samizdat Blog.

RUTH AWAD has an MFA in Creative Writing from Southern Illinois University Carbondale, and her work has appeared or is forthcoming in *The New Republic*, *Southern Indiana Review*, *CALYX*, *diode*, *Anti-*, *Rattle*, *The Missouri Review*'s Poem of the Week, *Vinyl Poetry*, *Epiphany*, *The Drunken Boat*, *Copper Nickel*, and elsewhere. She won the 2013 and 2012 Dorothy Sargent Rosenberg Poetry Prize and the 2011 Copper Nickel Poetry Contest. She was also a finalist for the 2013 Ruth Lilly Fellowship. She lives in Columbus, Ohio, with her two Pomeranians.

DAVID BAKER is Professor of English and holds the Thomas B. Fordham Chair of Creative Writing at Denison University. He is author of eleven books of poetry, most recently *Scavenger Loop* (2015, W. W. Norton) and *Never-Ending Birds* (Norton), which won the Theodore Roethke Memorial Poetry Prize in 2011. His five prose books include *Show Me Your Environment: Essays on Poetry, Poets, and Poems* (2014, Michigan) and *Radiant Lyre: Essays on Lyric Poetry* (2007, Graywolf, with Ann Townsend). Baker's poems and essays have appeared widely in such magazines as *American Poetry Review*, *The Atlantic Monthly*, *The Nation*, *The New Republic*, *The New Yorker*, *The Paris Review*, *Poetry*, *Slate*, and *The Yale Review*. For his work he has received fellowships and awards from the John Simon Guggenheim Memorial Foundation, the National Endowment for the Arts, the Poetry Society of America, the Ohio Arts Council, and the Society of Midland Authors.

HADARA BAR-NADAV is the author of *Lullaby (with Exit Sign)* (Saturnalia Books, 2013), awarded the Saturnalia Books Poetry Prize; *The Frame Called Ruin* (New Issues, 2012), Runner Up for the Green Rose Prize; and *A Glass of Milk to Kiss Goodnight* (Margie/Intuit House, 2007), awarded the Margie Book Prize.

Her chapbook, *Show Me Yours* (*Laurel Review*/Green Tower Press, 2010), was awarded the Midwest Poets Series Prize. She is also co-author of the textbook *Writing Poems*, 8th ed. (Pearson, 2011). Recent awards include the 2013 Lynda Hull Memorial Poetry Prize from *Crazyhorse* and fellowships from the Vermont Studio Center and the Virginia Center for the Creative Arts. Hadara is currently an Associate Professor of English at the University of Missouri-Kansas City.

MELISSA BARRETT's poems have recently appeared in *Gulf Coast*, *Anti-*, *The Journal*, *Web Conjunctions*, and *Best New Poets 2013*. She won *Narrative*'s 2014 poetry contest and was a finalist for this year's Ruth Lilly and Dorothy Sargent Rosenberg Poetry Fellowships from the Poetry Foundation. A recipient of an Ohio Arts Council Individual Excellence Award, a *Tin House* writer's scholarship, and a Galway Kinnell scholarship from the Community of Writers at Squaw Valley, she lives in Columbus, Ohio, and teaches at an urban public middle school.

MICAH BATEMAN is a poet from Iowa City, Iowa, where he teaches and works for the University of Iowa's International Writing Program. He's received awards and fellowships from Washington University in St. Louis, the Iowa Writers' Workshop, and the Poetry Society of America. His poems have been anthologized in *Privacy Policy: The Anthology of Surveillance Poetics* and *The Poet's Quest for God: 21st Century Poems of Faith, Doubt, and Wonder*.

JEFFREY BEAN is Associate Professor of English/Creative Writing at Central Michigan University. He is author of the poetry collection *Diminished Fifth* (WordTech) and the chapbook *Girl Reading a Letter at an Open Window* (Southeast Missouri State University Press), winner of the 2013 Vern Cowles/Copperdome

Poetry Chapbook Prize. Recent poems appear or are forthcoming in the journals *River Styx*, *Southern Poetry Review*, *Cimarron Review*, *Willow Springs*, *Smartish Pace*, and *Barn Owl Review*, among others.

ROY BENTLEY's work has been recognized with fellowships from the NEA, the Florida Division of Cultural Affairs, and the Ohio Arts Council. Poems have appeared in *The Southern Review*, *Shenandoah*, *Pleiades*, *Blackbird*, *North American Review*, *Prairie Schooner*, *American Literary Review*, and elsewhere. He has published four books of poetry: *Boy in a Boat* (University of Alabama, 1986), *Any One Man* (Bottom Dog Books, 1992), *The Trouble with a Short Horse in Montana* (White Pine Press, 2006), and *Starlight Taxi* (Lynx House Press, 2013). These days, he lives in Ohio.

MONICA BERLIN & BETH MARZONI's collaborations have appeared or are forthcoming in *Better: Culture & Lit*, *Boston Review*, *Colorado Review*, *Denver Quarterly*, *DIAGRAM*, *Meridian*, *New Orleans Review*, & *Water~Stone Review*, among others. Their book, *No Shape Bends the River So Long*, won the 2013 New Measure Poetry Prize and is forthcoming from Free Verse Editions at Parlor Press.

JENNIFER JACKSON BERRY is the author of the chapbooks *When I Was a Girl* (Sundress Publications, 2014) and *Nothing but Candy* (Liquid Paper Press, 2003). Her poems have appeared or are forthcoming in *Booth*, *The Emerson Review*, *Harpur Palate*, *Stirring*, and *Whiskey Island*, among others. A graduate of Indiana University's MFA program, she lives in Pittsburgh, Pennsylvania.

JASON BREDLE is the author of four books, most recently *Carnival,* selected as an Editor's Choice for the Akron Series in Poetry and published in September 2012 by the University of Akron Press.

RICHARD CECIL is the author of four collections of poetry, the most recent of which is *Twenty-First Century Blues* (Southern Illinois University Press, 2004). He teaches at Indiana University, Bloomington.

GEORGE DAVID CLARK teaches poetry at Valparaiso University. His *Reveille* (University of Arkansas Press) won the Miller Williams Prize in 2014 and his most recent poems can be found in new issues of *Alaska Quarterly Review, The Believer, Blackbird, FIELD, The Missouri Review, The Yale Review,* and elsewhere. He is the editor of *32 Poems* and lives in Indiana with his wife and their three young children.

SARAH COURY has worked as a small business owner, field biologist, and park ranger. Her poetry, prose, and nonfiction have appeared in a number of literary journals. She lives with her family in Kalamazoo, Michigan.

CATIE CRABTREE is a doctoral candidate in Literature and Creative Writing at the University of Utah. Her work has appeared in *Phoebe, The Laurel Review,* and elsewhere.

KAREN CRAIGO teaches English to international students at Drury University in Springfield, Missouri. A chapbook, *Someone Could Build Something Here,* was just published by Winged City Chapbook Press, and her previous chapbook, *Stone for an Eye,* is part of the Wick Poetry Series. Her work has appeared in the journals *Atticus Review, Poetry, Indiana Review, Prairie Schooner, Puerto del Sol, The MacGuffin,* and others.

CALEB CURTISS's writing has appeared in, or is forthcoming from, numerous literary journals including *New England Review, Passages North,* and *TriQuarterly.* Last year he was named a finalist for a Ruth Lilly Poetry Fellowship. He lives in Champaign, Illinois, where he teaches high school English, edits poetry for *Hobart,* and helps organize and curate the Pygmalion Literary Festival.

PAT DANEMAN has published fiction and poetry widely in print and online journals. Recent work appears in *Moon City Review, I-70 Review, Bellevue Poetry Review, Stone Canoe,* and *The Comstock Review.* Her chapbook, *Where the World Begins,* is forthcoming from Finishing Line Press. She is senior poetry editor of *Kansas City Voices* magazine and lives in Lenexa, Kansas.

STEVE DAVENPORT is the author of two poetry collections: *Overlook* (2012) and *Uncontainable Noise* (2006). His poems, stories, and essays have been anthologized, reprinted, and published in scores of literary magazines both online and in print. One of his stories received a 2011 Pushcart Prize Special Mention. His *Murder on Gasoline Lake,* available as a New American Press chapbook, is listed as Notable in Best American Essays 2007. He keeps a website/blog at http://gasolinelake.com.

PETER DAVIS writes, draws, and makes music in Muncie, Indiana. His books of poetry are *TINA* (Bloof Books, 2013), *Poetry! Poetry! Poetry!* (Bloof Books, 2010), and *Hitler's Mustache* (Barnwood Press, 2006). He edited *Poet's Bookshelf:*

Contemporary Poets on Books That Shaped Their Art (2005) and co-edited a second volume, *Poet's Bookshelf II* (2008). His poems have appeared in such places as *Jacket*, *La Petite Zine*, *Court Green*, *Rattle*, and *The Best American Poetry*. He lives with his lovely wife and two lovely children, and teaches at Ball State University. More info at artisnecessary.com.

Born in Ghana and raised in Jamaica, KWAME DAWES is the award-winning author of nineteen books of poetry, and numerous works of fiction, drama, criticism and non-fiction. His most recent book is *Duppy Conqueror: New and Selected Poems*. Dawes is the Glenna Luschei Editor of *Prairie Schooner*, a Chancellor's Professor of English at the University of Nebraska, and a faculty member of the Pacific MFA Program. Dawes is also the associate poetry editor at Peepal Tree Press and the director and supervising of the African Poetry Book Fund.

REBECCA DUNHAM is a Professor of English at the University of Wisconsin-Milwaukee. Her most recent collection of poems, *Glass Armonica* (Milkweed Editions 2013) won the Lindquist & Vennum Prize, which is awarded to an upper Midwest poet. Her two previous collections of poetry are *The Flight Cage* (Tupelo Press 2010) and *The Miniature Room* (Truman State University Press 2006). Although she is originally from New England, she definitely views herself as a Midwestern writer. She earned her Ph.D. in creative writing at the University of Missouri-Columbia and was the Jay C. and Ruth Halls Fellow in Poetry at the Wisconsin Institute of Creative Writing in 2005-2006. She has also received an NEA fellowship and her poems have appeared in journals such as *FIELD*, *The Antioch Review*, *Third Coast*, and *The Iowa Review*, among others. She will be the Distinguished Visiting Writer at Bowling Green State University in Spring 2015.

KATHY FAGAN's fifth collection of poems, *Sycamore*, will be published by Milkweed in 2016. New work is appearing in *FIELD*, *Narrative*, *Ninth Letter*, *The Kenyon Review*, and *Poetry*. Fagan teaches at Ohio State and serves as Series Editor of the OSU Press/The Journal Wheeler Poetry Prize. Visit her at http:// www.kathyfagan.net.

RICHARD FOX has contributed work to many literary journals. *Swagger & Remorse*, his first book of poetry, was published in December 2007. He received a full fellowship for poetry from the Illinois Arts Council. He holds a BFA in Photography from Tyler School of Art, Philadelphia, and lives in Chicago.

MARC J. FRAZIER has been widely published in journals including *The Spoon River Poetry Review*, *ACM*, *Caveat Lector*, *Slant*, *Permafrost*, *Plainsongs*, *Poet Lore*, *Rhino*, *The Broome Review*, *descant*, and *The G W Review*. He is the recipient of an Illinois Arts Council Award for poetry. His book *The Way Here* and his chapbooks *The Gods of the Grand Resort* and *After* are available on Amazon. His second full-length collection, *Each Thing Touches*, is forthcoming from Glass Lyre Press in June 2015. His website is www.marcfrazier.org.

STEPHEN FRECH has published three volumes of poetry: *Toward Evening and the Day Far Spent* (Kent State University Press) won the 1995 Wick Poetry Chapbook Contest; *If Not For These Wrinkles of Darkness* won the White Pine Press Poetry Prize, published in 2001; and *The Dark Villages of Childhood* won the 2008 Mississippi Valley Poetry Chapbook Prize. He has a fourth volume titled *A Palace of Strangers Is No City*, a sustained narrative of prose poetry/flash fiction, published by Cervena Barva Press in 2011. His translation from the Dutch of Menno

Wigman's book of poems *Zwart als kaviaar/Black as Caviar* was published in 2012. He has been the recipient of the Elliston Poetry Writing Fellowship, the Milton Center Post-Graduate Writing Fellowship, and grants from the Ludwig Vogelstein Foundation and the Illinois Arts Council. He is founder and editor of Oneiros Press, and an Associate Professor of English at Millikin University.

JOHN GALLAHER is, together with G.C. Waldrep, the author of *Your Father on the Train of Ghosts*, which was written in collaboration almost completely through email. Gallaher's previous collections of poetry include *The Little Book of Guesses* (2007), winner of the Levis Poetry Prize, and *Map of the Folded World* (2009). His work has appeared in such journals as *FIELD, Denver Quarterly, Ploughshares, New American Writing, Colorado Review,* and *The Kenyon Review,* as well as in *The Best American Poetry 2008.* In 2010, he won the *Boston Review* Poetry Prize. He is currently co-editor of *The Laurel Review,* and, with Mary Biddinger, the Akron Series in Contemporary Poetics. Gallaher's latest work, *In a Landscape* (BOA, 2014), is a book-length essay-poem and can be ordered through the BOA Bookstore.

BRANDI GEORGE grew up in rural Michigan. Her first collection of poetry, *Gog,* is forthcoming from Black Lawrence Press in 2015. Poems from this manuscript have appeared in such journals as *Gulf Coast, Prairie Schooner, Ninth Letter,* and *The Iowa Review.* She currently resides in Tallahassee, where she is a PhD candidate at Florida State University.

TYLER GOBBLE is editor-in-chief of *NOÖ Journal,* chapbook editor for Magic Helicopter Press, and the host of Everything Is Bigger, a reading series in Austin, Texas. He is currently a poetry fellow in the Michener Center for Writers. He has plopped out a chunk of chapbooks, most recently *Collected Feelings with Layne Ransom* (Forklift INK). He likes disc golf, tank tops, and bacon. More at www.tylergobble.com.

CHRIS GREEN is the author of two books of poetry: *Epiphany School* and *The Sky over Walgreens*. His poetry has appeared in such journals as *Poetry, Verse, Court Green, North American Review,* and *Rattle*. He edited the anthology, *A Writers' Congress: Chicago Poets on Barack Obama's Inauguration* and is co-editor of *Brute Neighbors: Urban Nature Poetry, Prose & Photography*. A graduate of Bennington College's MFA program, he teaches in the English Department at DePaul University.

Originally from the flatlands of central Illinois, JUSTIN HAMM now lives near Twain territory in Missouri. He is the founding editor of *the museum of americana* and the author of a full-length collection of poems, *Lessons in Ruin* (Aldrich Press, 2014), as well as two poetry chapbooks, *Illinois, My Apologies* (RockSaw Press, 2011) and *The Everyday Parade/Alone With Turntable, Old Records* (Crisis Chronicles Press, 2013). His poems or stories have appeared, or will soon appear, in *Nimrod, The New York Quarterly, Cream City Review, Punchnel's, Hobart, Sugar House Review,* and a host of other publications. Recent work has also been selected for the Stanley Hanks Memorial Poetry Prize from the St. Louis Poetry Center.

DENNIS HINRICHSEN is the author of seven books of poetry. His most recent is *Skin Music,* co-winner of the 2014 Michael Waters Poetry Prize from Southern Indiana Review Press and forthcoming in summer 2015. His previous books include *Riptooth* (2010 Tampa Poetry Prize) and *Kurosawa's Dog* (2008

FIELD Poetry Prize). An earlier work, *Detail from The Garden of Earthly Delights*, received the 1999 Akron Poetry Prize. He lives in Lansing, Michigan.

AMORAK HUEY is author of the chapbook *The Insomniac Circus* (Hyacinth Girl Press, 2014) and the forthcoming poetry collection *Ha Ha Ha Thump* (Sundress Publications, 2015). A former newspaper editor and reporter, he teaches writing at Grand Valley State University in Michigan. His poems appear in *The Best American Poetry 2012*, *The Cincinnati Review*, *The Southern Review*, *The Collagist*, *Menacing Hedge*, and many other print and online journals. Follow him on Twitter:@amorak.

ROCHELLE HURT is the author of *The Rusted City* (White Pine, 2014). An Ohio native, she was born in Dayton, raised in Youngstown, and currently lives in Cincinnati. Her work has been included in *Best New Poets 2013*, and she has been awarded literary prizes from *Crab Orchard Review*, *Arts & Letters*, *Hunger Mountain*, and *Poetry International*. Her poetry, fiction, and creative nonfiction have been published in journals like *Mid-American Review*, *Cincinnati Review*, *The Southeast Review*, *The Kenyon Review Online*, and *Image*.

LIAM HYSJULIEN's poetry has appeared in *The New Republic*, the *American Reader*, *All Hollow*, the *Brooklyn Quarterly*, *MAYDAY Magazine*, and elsewhere.

RICH IVES has received grants and awards from the National Endowment for the Arts, Artist Trust, Seattle Arts Commission, and the Coordinating Council of Literary Magazines for his work in poetry, fiction, editing, publishing, translation, and photography. His writing has appeared in *Verse, North American*

Review, *Massachusetts Review*, *Northwest Review*, *Quarterly West*, *The Iowa Review*, *Poetry Northwest*, *Virginia Quarterly Review*, *Fiction Daily*, and many more. He is the 2009 winner of the Francis Locke Memorial Poetry Award from *Bitter Oleander*. His story collection, *The Balloon Containing the Water Containing the Narrative Begins Leaking*, was one of five finalists for the 2009 Starcherone Innovative Fiction Prize. He has received a nomination for *The Best of the Web* and nominations for both the Pushcart Prize and The Best of the Net. Ives is the 2012 winner of the Creative Nonfiction Prize from *Thin Air* magazine. The Spring 2011 *Bitter Oleander* contains a feature including an interview and eighteen of his hybrid works.

SEAN KARNS is the author of the poetry collection *Jar of Pennies* (New American Press, 2015). His poetry has appeared in *Hobart* (web), *Rattle*, *Pleiades*, *Los Angeles Review*, *Cold Mountain Review*, *Folio*, *MAYDAY Magazine*, and elsewhere.

NATHAN KEMP is an associate editor for *Whiskey Island*, a poetry editor for *Barn Owl Review*, and a staff reviewer for *American Microreviews and Interviews*. His work appears or is forthcoming in *Bodega*, *Columbia Poetry Review*, *H_NGM_N*, and *South Dakota Review*. He lives in Akron, Ohio.

JESSE LEE KERCHEVAL is the author of fourteen books, including the memoir *Space* (University of Wisconsin Press, 2014) and the book-length Spanish language poem *Torres* (Editorial Yaugarú, 2014.) She is the editor of *América invertida: an anthology of younger Uruguayan poets*, forthcoming from the University of New Mexico Press.

JOSHUA KLEINBERG was born in 1989 in South Florida and moved with his family to Canton, Ohio, when he was ten years old. A high school dropout, he attended Cleveland State and the University of Montana before graduating from Ohio State, where he was the recipient of an Academy of American Poets Prize. He has worked as part of the Monster House Press collective in Columbus, Ohio; at The Blueberry House, a diy showspace in Akron; and as the Ohio News Editor for *Coldfront Magazine*. His work has appeared in places like *Spork*; *Artifice*; *Forklift, Ohio*; *The Southeast Review*; and in the anthology *Chorus: A Literary Mixtape* (2012, MTV Books). He lives currently in New York, where he attends the MFA in Poetry at Columbia University and serves as co-curator (with Dana Jaye Cadman) of Banquet Reading Series in Brooklyn.

DANIEL LASSELL won a William J. Maier Writing Award in 2013 and has been featured, or is forthcoming, in publications such as *Steam Ticket Journal*, *Future Cycle*, *3Elements Review*, *Reed Magazine*, *Haiku Journal*, and *Sixfold*. In his youth, he raised llamas on a farm in Eminence, Kentucky. Today, he lives with his wife in Indianapolis, Indiana.

LYN LIFSHIN is the author of more than 100 books, and her work has appeared in such journals as *American Poetry Review*, *Another Chicago Magazine*, *Georgia Review*, *The Iowa Review*, *The Literary Review*, *New York Quarterly*, and *Ploughshares*, among many others. "Thirty Miles West of Chicago" is included in *A Girl Goes into the Woods: Selected Poems*, and is reprinted in this anthology by permission of the author.

SANDY LONGHORN is the author of three books of poetry, *The Alchemy of My Mortal Form* (forthcoming from Trio House Press), *The Girlhood Book of Prairie Myths* (Jacar Press), and *Blood Almanac* (Anhinga Press). Recent poems have appeared in *Hayden's Ferry Review*, *Hotel Amerika*, *The Southeast Review*,

Tupelo Quarterly, and elsewhere. Longhorn teaches at Pulaski Technical College, where she directs the Big Rock Reading Series, and for the online MFA Program at the University of Arkansas Monticello. In addition, she co-edits the online journal *Heron Tree* and blogs at *Myself the Only Kangaroo among the Beauty*.

KIM LOZANO lives in St. Louis, Missouri, and teaches creative writing for Oasis, a lifelong learning organization for adults age fifty and older. She serves as a contributing editor at *River Styx* and also co-directs the River Styx at the Tavern reading series. Her work has been published or is forthcoming in *Poetry Daily*, *The Iowa Review*, *Alaska Quarterly Review*, *The Journal*, *Denver Quarterly*, *Valparaiso Poetry Review*, *Midwestern Gothic*, *The Pinch*, the anthology *Discoveries: New Writing from The Iowa Review*, and elsewhere.

SANDRA MARCHETTI is the author of *Confluence*, a debut full-length collection of poetry from Sundress Publications. Eating Dog Press also published an illustrated edition of her essays and poetry, *A Detail in the Landscape*, and her first volume, *The Canopy*, won Midwest Writing Center's Mississippi Valley Chapbook Contest. Sandy won Second Prize in *Prick of the Spindle*'s 2014 Poetry Open Competition and her work appears in *The Journal*, *Subtropics*, *The Hollins Critic*, *Sugar House Review*, *Mid-American Review*, *Thrush Poetry Journal*, *Green Mountains Review*, *South Dakota Review*, *Appalachian Heritage*, *Southwest Review*, *Prairie Gold: An Anthology of the American Heartland*, and elsewhere. She lives and works outside of Chicago.

ADRIAN MATEJKA is the author of *The Devil's Garden*, winner of the New York / New England Award, and *Mixology*, which was a winner of the 2008 National Poetry Series. His most recent collection of poems, *The Big Smoke*, was awarded the 2014

Anisfield-Wolf Prize and was a finalist for the 2013 National Book Award and 2014 Pulitzer Prize. He is the recipient of fellowships from *Cave Canem*, the Guggenheim Foundation, and the Lannan Foundation. He teaches creative writing and literature at Indiana University in Bloomington.

CARLO MATOS has published four books of poetry. His new book, *The Secret Correspondence of Loon and Fiasco*, is forthcoming from Mayapple Press. He has also published poems, stories, and essays in *The Iowa Review*, *PANK*, *Another Chicago Magazine*, *DIAGRAM*, and *The Gavea-Brown Book of Portuguese-American Poetry*, among many others. Carlo has received grants from the Illinois Arts Council and the Fundação Luso-Americana (FLAD). He lives in Chicago, where he teaches at the City Colleges of Chicago and the Rooster Moans Poetry Coop. A former fighter, he now trains and coaches cage fighters and kickboxers. After hours he can be found entertaining clients at the Chicago Poetry Bordello and writing poems on demand with Poems While You Wait. He blogs at carlomatos.blogspot. com. Follow him on twitter @CarloMatos46.

ZACHARIAH MCVICKER is an MFA candidate at the University of Illinois at Urbana-Champaign. Before graduate school, he received his BA in English Literature from The Ohio State University while working as a line cook in Columbus and was a fellow at the Bucknell Seminar for Younger Poets. He has been published in the *Birmingham Poetry Review* and *32 Poems*. He currently works at the Illinois Natural History Survey hunting rootworm beetles in the cornfields.

TREY MOODY is the author of *Thought That Nature* (Sarabande Books, 2014), winner of the Kathryn A. Morton Prize in Poetry. He earned his PhD at the University of Nebraska-Lincoln.

MATTHEW MURRAY's poems have appeared in *Tar River Poetry*, *Poetry East*, and *Rattle*. He has received an NEA Fellowship in Poetry. He worked as a mental health clinician for many years but is now a high school librarian. He lives in Urbana, Illinois, with his partner; they have two grown sons who live in the Pacific Northwest.

RICHARD NEWMAN is the author of the poetry collections *All the Wasted Beauty of the World* (Able Muse Press, 2014), *Domestic Fugues* (Steel Toe Books, 2009), and *Borrowed Towns* (Word Press, 2005). His poems have appeared in *Best American Poetry*, *Boulevard*, *Crab Orchard Review*, *New Letters*, *The Sun*, and many other periodicals and anthologies, and have been featured many times on Garrison Keillor's *Writer's Almanac*, Ted Kooser's *American Life in Poetry*, *Poetry Daily*, and *Verse Daily*. He lives in St. Louis, where he serves as editor of *River Styx*, co-directs the River Styx at the Tavern reading series, and plays in the junkfolk band The CharFlies.

ANDREW NICHOLSON's poems have appeared in magazines and journals including *Colorado Review*, *Eleven Eleven*, and *Spinning Jenny*. In the summer of 2013, he was an Artist-in-Residence at the Palazzo Rinaldi in Noepoli, Italy. He is currently working on translations of the French poet, Pierre Reverdy. He joined the English Department at UNLV in 2013.

DEONTE OSAYANDE is a poet, essayist and performer from Detroit, Michigan. His works have appeared in over a dozen publications, including *Camroc Press Review*, *Front Porch Review*, and *Prime Number Magazine*. He's a two-time member of the Detroit National Poetry Slam Team and a Pushcart Prize nominee. He teaches creative writing for Wayne County

Community College District and the Inside Out Detroit Literary Arts Project.

RACHAEL PECKHAM is the author of the chapbook *Muck Fire* (Spring Garden Press) and the recipient of the 2010 Robert Watson Poetry Award. Her work recently received a Pushcart Prize nomination and "Notable Mention" in the *2012 Best American Essays* collection. Her prose poems have appeared widely in places like *Brevity, Dos Passos Review, Gulf Coast, Edge, Sentence, South Loop Review*, and in the anthology *Not Somewhere Else but Here: A Contemporary Anthology of Women & Place* (Sundress 2014).

JAN PETTIT's writing has appeared in numerous publications, including *Water~Stone Review, Cream City Review, Tusculum Review, Natural Bridge*, and an anthology of poets from Nebraska, *Nebraska Presence*. She was co-winner of the Bill Holm: Winter in Variations Poetry Contest and has been featured on the MnArtists.org audio segment, *You Are Hear*. Jan is a graduate of the MFA Program at Hamline University and lives in Minneapolis.

MIKE PUICAN has had poetry in *Poetry, Michigan Quarterly Review*, and *New England Review*, among others. His reviews have appeared in *The Kenyon Review, Another Chicago Magazine*, and *TriQuarterly*. He won the 2004 Tia Chucha Press Chapbook Contest for his chapbook, *30 Seconds*. Mike was a member of the 1996 Chicago Slam Team and for the past eight years has been president of the board of the Guild Literary Complex.

MARY QUADE is the author of *Guide to Native Beasts* (Cleveland State University Poetry Center). She has received two Ohio Arts

Council Individual Excellence Awards for poetry (2006, 2010) and one for prose (2014). Her poems have appeared in anthologies including *On the Wing: American Poems of Air and Space Flight* (University of Iowa) and *New Voices: Contemporary Poetry from the United States* (Irish Pages), published as part of the National Endowment for the Arts International Exchange program. She lives in rural northeast Ohio is an Associate Professor of English at Hiram College.

LAYNE RANSOM was born and raised in southern Indiana, and attended Ball State University in Muncie, Indiana. She has been published in *Big Lucks*; *Forklift, Ohio*; *elimae*; and others. Her chapbook *You Are the Meat* was released in 2013 from H_NGM_N. She is currently an MFA candidate in poetry at the New Writers Project in Austin, Texas.

NANCY REDDY is the author of *Double Jinx* (Milkweed Editions, 2015), winner of the 2014 National Poetry Series. Her poems have most recently appeared in *Tupelo Quarterly*, *32 Poems*, and *Smartish Pace*.

MARGARET ROSS earned her M.F.A. at the Iowa Writers' Workshop in 2011 and has taught at the University of Iowa, Cornell College, and the International Writing Program. Her poetry has been recognized with an Iowa Arts Fellowship, a Fulbright grant, and scholarships from the Bread Loaf Writers' Conference. Her first book, *A Timeshare*, will be published by Omnidawn in 2015.

MARY KAY RUMMEL is poet laureate of Ventura County, California. Her seventh book of poetry, *The Lifeline Trembles*, has been published by Blue Light Press as a winner of the 2014 Blue Light Poetry Prize. She is a professor emerita from the University of Minnesota, Duluth and teaches part time at California State University, Channel Islands, dividing her time between California and Minneapolis.

JUSTIN RUNGE lives in Lawrence, Kansas, where he serves as poetry editor of *Parcel*. He is the author of two chapbooks, *Plainsight* (New Michigan Press, 2012) and *Hum Decode* (Greying Ghost Press, 2014). Recipient of a 2014 Lawrence Arts Center Langston Hughes Award, Runge has published in *Linebreak*, *DIAGRAM*, *Harpur Palate*, *Best New Poets 2013*, and elsewhere. He can be found at www.justinrunge.me.

NATALIE SHAPERO is the author of *No Object* (Saturnalia, 2013), and her writing has appeared in *The Believer*, *The New Republic*, *The New Yorker*, *Poetry*, *The Progressive*, and elsewhere. She lives in Columbus, Ohio, and works as an associate editor at *The Kenyon Review*.

PHILIPPE SHILS lives in Decatur, Illinois, where he works as a physician assistant. His poems can be read in *Rattle*, *Sixth Finch*, *2River View*, *BODY*, *Right Hand Pointing*, *Alba*, *Metazen*, and others. He is a member of the New New Pennies Massive, an online writing workshop.

MAGGIE SMITH is the author of *The Well Speaks of Its Own Poison* (Tupelo Press, 2015), winner of the Dorset Prize; *Lamp of the Body* (Red Hen Press), winner of the Benjamin Saltman Poetry Award; and three chapbooks: *The List of Dangers* (Kent State), *Nesting Dolls* (Pudding House), and the forthcoming *Disasterology* (Dream Horse Press). The grateful recipient of fellowships from the National Endowment for the Arts, the Ohio Arts Council, and the Sustainable Arts Foundation, Smith lives in Bexley, Ohio, and works as a freelance writer and editor.

ROBERT STEWART won a National Magazine Award in 2008 for editorial achievement in the essay category (he was a finalist for that award in 2007) from the American Society of Magazine Editors. Poems have appeared in *The Iowa Review*, *Denver Quarterly*, *Poetry Northwest*, *Prairie Schooner*, *Miramar*, *Stand*, *Notre Dame Review*, *The Literary Review*, and other magazines. Books include *The Narrow Gate: Writing, Art & Values* (essays, Serving House Books, 2014), *Outside Language: Essays* (Helicon Nine Editions, a finalist in the PEN Center USA Literary Awards for 2004; and winner of the 2004 Thorpe Menn Award), *Plumbers* (poems, BkMk Press), and others. He is editor of *New Letters* magazine, BkMk Press, and *New Letters on the Air*, a nationally syndicated literary radio program at the University of Missouri-Kansas City.

JESSICA D. THOMPSON's poetry has appeared in *Appalachian Heritage*, *Atlanta Review*, *The Midwest Quarterly*, *The Sow's Ear Poetry Review*, and *Tiferet Journal*, among others. She is the grateful recipient of *New Southerner*'s 2013 James Baker Hall Memorial Prize in Poetry and the 2014 Kudzu Poetry Prize. Her poetry chapbook *Bullets and Blank Bibles* was published by Liquid Paper Press in 2013. She was also a finalist in *Ruminate Magazine*'s 2014 Janet B. McCabe Poetry Prize.

JEFF TIGCHELAAR's poems have appeared in journals and anthologies including *LIT*, *The Laurel Review*, *North American Review*, *Rhino*, *Hunger Mountain*, *Sand*, *The Offending Adam*, *Best New Poets 2011*, and *Verse Daily*. His blog, "Stay-at-Home Pop Culture," is published by *XYZ Magazine*, and his poetry collection, *Certain Streets at an Uncertain Hour*, is from Woodley Press (2014).

LEE UPTON is the author of *The Tao of Humiliation: Stories*, which was released from BOA Editions in May, 2014. She is the author of twelve other books, including the essay collection *Swallowing the Sea: On Writing & Ambition Boredom Purity & Secrecy*; the novella *The Guide to the Flying Island*; and a fifth collection of poetry, *Undid in the Land of Undone*. She is a professor of English and the writer-in-residence at Lafayette College.

WENDY VARDAMAN is the author of *Obstructed View* (Fireweed Press), co-editor of *Echolocations, Poets Map Madison* (Cowfeather Press), co-editor of *Verse Wisconsin* (versewisconsin. org), and co-founder of Cowfeather Press (cowfeatherpress.org). She teaches independently and through the Loft Literary Center and the UW-Madison's Division of Continuing Studies, organizes community events and conversations about poetry, and writes essays and interviews, which have appeared in *Poetry Daily*, *Women's Review of Books*, Poets.org, and other venues, including her blog, *live art(s) art live(s)* (wvar-daman.tumblr.com). She has a Ph.D. in English from the University of Pennsylvania and was named is one of two Poets Laureates named by Madison, Wisconsin (2012-2015). With husband, Thomas DuBois, she has three adult children and has never owned a car.

The poems of LISA VIHOS have appeared in *Big Muddy*, *The Camel Saloon*, *Forge*, *Main Street Rag*, *Red Cedar*, *Red Fez*, *Seems*, *Verse Wisconsin*, *Wisconsin People and Ideas*, and *Your Daily Poem*. She has two Pushcart Prize Nominations and two chapbooks: *A Brief History of Mail* (Pebblebrook Press, 2011) and *The Accidental Present* (Finishing Line Press, 2012). She is the Poetry and Arts Editor of *Stoneboat* and an occasional guest blogger for *The Best American Poetry*. She is originally from

Chicago and currently lives in Sheboygan, Wisconsin, where she enjoys Lake Michigan, cooking, hiking, reading, and listening to her teenage son play guitar. She keeps a blog of poetry and prose musings called *Frying the Onion* at http://lisavihos.wordpress.com.

ANGELA VORAS-HILLS earned her MFA at UMass-Boston and was a fellow at the Writers' Room of Boston. Her work has appeared in *Kenyon Review Online*, *Best New Poets*, *Hayden's Ferry Review*, and *Linebreak*, among others. She was recently awarded the Sustainable Arts Foundation's Spring Promise Award and lives with her husband and two kids in Madison, WI.

DONNA VORREYER is the author of *A House of Many Windows* (Sundress Publications, 2013). Her work has appeared in many journals including *Rhino, Linebreak, Cider Press Review, Stirring, Sweet, wicked alice,* and *Weave*. Her fifth chapbook, *We Build Houses of Our Bodies*, was released in late 2013 by Dancing Girl Press, and her second poetry collection is forthcoming from Sundress Publications in 2016.

For the last thirty years, JOE WEINTRAUB has published a variety of fiction, essays, poetry, and translations in all sorts of literary reviews and periodicals, from *The Massachusetts Review* to *Modern Philology*, from *Gastronomica* to *Prairie Schooner*. Many of his pieces have been anthologized, and he is a recipient of Illinois Arts Council Awards for fiction and creative nonfiction. He's been an Around-the-Coyote poet, a StoneSong poet, and has had one-act plays produced by the Theatre-Studio in New York City, the Summer Place Theatre in Naperville, IL, and Theatre One in Middleboro, MA. He is currently a network playwright at Chicago Dramatists.

MARK WILLIAMS is retired from the real estate business in Evansville, Indiana, where he lives with his wife, DeeGee. His writing has appeared in *The Hudson Review*, *Indiana Review*, *The Southern Review*, *Open 24 Hours*, *Nimrod*, and *Rattle*. His poem, "In the Blue Box," appears in the e-book anthology, *The Burden of Light: Poems on Illness and Loss*; and Finishing Line Press will publish his long poem, "Happiness," as a chapbook in December. His crepe myrtle blooms are pink.

THERESA WILLIAMS is the author of the novel, *The Secret of Hurricanes*. Her novel-in-stories, *Blue Velvis*, is forthcoming from Shebooks. Her stories and poems have appeared in many magazines, including *Chattahoochee Review*, *Gargoyle*, *Hunger Mountain*, and *The Sun*. She is currently working on a graphic novel called *The Wanderers*.

EDITOR
BIOGRAPHIES

OKLA ELLIOTT is an Illinois Distinguished Fellow at the University of Illinois where he works in the fields of comparative literature and trauma studies. He also holds an MFA from Ohio State University. His nonfiction, poetry, short fiction, and translations have appeared in *Another Chicago Magazine, Harvard Review, Indiana Review, The Literary Review, New York Quarterly, Prairie Schooner, A Public Space,* and *Subtropics,* among others. His books include *From the Crooked Timber* (short fiction), *The Cartographer's Ink* (poetry), and *The Doors You Mark Are Your Own* (a novel co-authored with Raul Clement). His book of translation, *Blackbirds in September: Selected Shorter Poems of Jürgen Becker,* is forthcoming in late 2015.

HANNAH STEPHENSON is a poet, editor, and instructor living in Columbus, Ohio (where she also runs a monthly literary event series called Paging Columbus). She is the author of *In the Kettle, the Shriek* (Gold Wake Press), editor of *The Ides of March: An Anthology of Ohio Poets* (Columbus Creative Cooperative), and a poetry and arts blogger for *The Huffington Post;* her writing has appeared in publications that include *The Atlantic, Hobart, 32 Poems, Sixth Finch, Poetry Daily,* and *The Nervous Breakdown.* You can visit her online at *The Storialist* (www.thestorialist.com).

2015 HEARTLAND POETRY PRIZE FINAL JUDGE

A Wyoming native and second-generation Japanese American, LEE ANN RORIPAUGH studied music, earning a BM in piano performance and an MM in music history before earning an MFA in creative writing from Indiana University, Bloomington. She is the author of *Beyond Heart Mountain* (1999), which was selected by Ishmael Reed for the National Poetry Series; *Year of the Snake* (2004); and *On the Cusp of a Dangerous Year* (2009). Roripaugh's awards include a Bush Artist Foundation Individual Fellowship and the 1995 Randall Jarrell International Poetry Prize.